Developing Arts-Loving Readers

Top 10 Questions Teachers Are Asking about Integrated Arts Education

Nan McDonald
Douglas Fisher

A SCARECROWEDUCATION BOOK

The Scarecrow Press, Inc.
Lanham, Maryland, and London
2002

A SCARECROWEDUCATION BOOK

Published in the United States of America
by Scarecrow Press, Inc.
A Member of the Rowman & Littlefield Publishing Group
4720 Boston Way, Lanham, Maryland 20706
www.scarecrowpress.com

4 Pleydell Gardens, Folkestone
Kent CT20 2DN, England

British Library Cataloguing in Publication Information Available

Library of Congress Cataloging-in-Publication Data

McDonald, Nan (Nan Leslie), 1950–
   Developing arts-loving readers : top 10 questions teachers are asking
about integrated arts education / Nan McDonald, Douglas Fisher.
          p. cm.
"A Scarecrow Education book."
Includes bibliographical references.
   ISBN 0-8108-4453-2 (alk. paper)—ISBN 0-8108-4309-9 (pbk. : alk. paper)
   1. Arts—Study and teaching (Elementary) 2. Language arts
(Elementary) 3. Interdisciplinary approach in education. I. Fisher,
Douglas, 1965– II. Title.
   LB1591 .M43 2002
   372.5—dc21

                                                  2002022374

♾™ The paper used in this publication meets the minimum requirements of
American National Standard for Information Sciences—Permanence of
Paper for Printed Library Materials, ANSI/NISO Z39.48-1992.
Manufactured in the United States of America.

To our mothers, our first teachers, who allowed
us to learn in all the ways we could. Thank you
Veronica Tish McDonald, Sandi Fisher,
and Donna Fisher.

Contents

Acknowledgments

Thanking all those responsible for making this book a reality is no easy task. Working as a team prevents anyone from truly "owning" an idea or an innovation. We built on each other's ideas, brainstormed to increasingly more complex levels, and looked to our colleagues for support, constructive criticism, and brutal honesty.

The ideas in this book have been tested in a number of ways. Many of the ideas in this book have been developed for use in classrooms in San Diego County—especially in the City Heights Educational Pilot Schools: Rosa Parks Elementary, Monroe Clark Middle, and Hoover High School. We appreciate the time that these teachers have allowed us into their classrooms and provided feedback on our ideas. In addition to classroom tests, many of the ideas in this book have been presented at conferences and in various publications. We appreciate the support of the California Music Educators Association and the California Reading Association for inviting us to share with teachers at their conferences. Many thanks to the editorial team at Scott Foresman/Silver Burdett Ginn Music for providing us an opportunity to correlate musical materials with our integrated arts lessons. In terms of publications, previous versions of some of the lesson plan ideas have appeared in the following:

Fisher, D., and McDonald, N. (2000). "'With stars in their eyes': An integrated arts unit on the night sky." *Telling Stories: Theory, Practice, Interviews and Reviews*, 4(2), 15–22.

Fisher, D., and McDonald, N. (2001). "The intersection between music and early literacy instruction: Listening to literacy." *Reading Improvement, 38, 106–115*.

McDonald, N., and Fisher, D. (1999). "Bug suites: An uncommonly integrated performance unit for fourth through eighth grade." *Telling Stories: Theory, Practice, Interviews and Reviews*, 3(2), 17–25.

McDonald, N., and Fisher, D. (2000). "Tell them I sing: A dialogue on integrating curricula." *General Music Today*, 14(1), 13–18.

McDonald, N., and Fisher, D. (2000). "Strings attached: An introductory unit in musical listening." *Music Educators Journal*, 88(5), 32–39.

McDondald, N., and Fisher, D. (2001–2002). "Movin' along: The poetry of transportation." *Telling Stories: Theory, Practice, Interviews and Reviews*, 6(1), 10–17.

We would also like to acknowledge our editors at Scarecrow Education, Tom Koerner and Cindy Tursman, for believing in us and our ideas, and moving us through the publication process. After we had their support, we turned to the colleagues with whom we have worked with most closely. Ian Pumpian deserves huge thanks for his role in City Heights and in making this book possible. His belief that together we can make a difference in the lives of our students has been a constant motivating force. We also wish to acknowledge the contribution of the artwork by Ryan Ott. We would like to give special thanks to our colleagues and friends who provided support and feedback during the writing of this book, including: Frank Almond, Martin Chambers, Nancy Frey, Charles Friedrichs, James Flood, Diane Lapp, and Caren Sax. This group of amazing individuals we are proud to call friends. And, of course, we must thank all the future teachers, who keep us grounded in what works and what needs to be changed in classrooms.

Finally, we would like to thank our families for their patience and support during the deadline crunches, the hours of writing, and agonizing over details. We are extremely fortunate to have such love.

CHAPTER 1

Why Should I Have Arts in My Classroom? Which Arts?

Every child is an artist. The problem is how to remain an artist once he grows up.

—Pablo Picasso

This chapter provides both rationale and support for arts instruction as core curriculum within elementary and middle school classroom environments and moves us toward an understanding and valuing of education in the arts: drama, music, dance, and visual art.

Those of us who have lost track of time as we stop to admire the color and detail of a wonderful painting or a luminescent piece of hand-blown glass, or have been willingly suspended in thought or stimulating conversation after taking in a particularly meaningful play, or been profoundly moved (though speechless) after hearing a beautiful piece of music—we know what art can mean to our lives. Many of us have also been fortunate enough to be educated in the arts (music, visual art, drama, and dance) and thereby provided with opportunities to actively participate in many art-making experiences.

We might literally live for moments when we can again immerse ourselves into various forms of art—either as a direct participant or as an appreciative and enlightened audience member. We learned to love art by valuing the artistry within ourselves and others. We do so because the arts lend powerful beauty, expression, mystery, and wonder to our lives. Experiences in the arts richly augment our ordinary life experiences and by doing so, often lead us to tacit understandings of the deeper meanings of our existence, our culture, and our world.

The purpose of this book is to explore reasons and provide direct models toward the development of arts-loving readers through instruction designed to enhance reading, writing, and oral language development in all children. Furthermore, our goal is the delivery of quality integrated arts education, which is purposely infused within and connected to other learning within the elementary and middle school. If we believe that an education in the arts is crucial to a child's development and understanding of the world, a primary goal should be to educate all of our children in the arts. Our experience suggests that this goal can be accomplished within purposeful integrated contexts where children's learning in the arts is vitally connected to other learning at hand, without sacrificing the integrity or worth of the arts as distinct discipline content areas.

Rather than replace or diminish the value of discipline-specific education in the arts, we seek to explore ways to augment children's education in the arts by increasing teacher interest and empowering more educators toward the delivery of integrated instruction to more children. The arts can become accessible to more teachers and students and contain valuable, unique, powerful, natural, and active ways of thinking, learning, and knowing in our classrooms. Through various kinds of planned, purposeful integrative activities, students can directly and actively experience natural, unforced, authentic, and valid connections between the arts and other disciplines, which are designed to enhance and augment students' understanding through meaningful learning activity. The proceeding chapters of this book explain purposeful arts integration and provide models toward these ends.

WHY ARTS?

As we know, the arts hold a respected place within our core curriculum and therefore contain specific and important content toward the development of educated human beings. As such, the arts also hold an esteemed role in the transmission and perpetuation of culture; therefore, knowledge about art is knowledge about many expressive mediums found within human existence. In his address at the Los Angeles Music Center, Charles Broudy commented on the universal importance and powerful communications found within the arts:

> What a culture deems important it enshrines in art. The origin of the tribe, its gods, tragedies, and victories are transformed into artistic images through legends, drama, sculpture, architecture, song, dance, and story. Without the images of art, these ideals and values cannot make a

lasting impact on the member of the culture; they are the memory of the culture. (Broudy, 1984)

Expanding upon the importance of the arts and the need for their strong presence within education, Ernest Boyer, president of the Carnegie Foundation for the Advancement of Teaching, commented, "The arts are one of mankind's most visual and essential forms of language, and if we do not educate our children in the symbol system called the arts, we will lose not only our culture and civility but our humanity as well" (quoted within California Department of Education, p. v). In light of today's challenge to fully and comprehensively educate all children, many of whom learn within struggling and volatile school environments, the need for increasing humanizing experiences within education simply cannot be argued.

Similarly, the writers of *National Standards for Arts Education* (MENC, 1994a) add, "If our civilization is to continue to be both dynamic and nurturing, its success will ultimately depend on how well we develop the capacities of our children, not only to earn a living in a vastly complex world, but to live a life rich in meaning. . . . No one can claim to be truly educated who lacks basic knowledge and skills in the arts" (p. 5). Furthermore, in light of current educational focus toward applications of technology to student learning experiences, the arts can play a significant role in linking students to the ideas used in creating that technology. Participation in the arts helps shape and preserve our culture and the technologies used within that culture. To this, Elliot Eisner commented:

> Because new technologies, when used in the construction of images make new demands on thinking, those demands have something important to do with one of our most significant educational concerns, *the invention of mind*. The kind of mind we come to own is profoundly influenced by what we have had an opportunity to learn and experience. The mind is a vast potentiality. The course of its development is shaped by use. Use, in turn, is shaped by the conditions of the culture in which one lives. When one shapes the culture, and schooling is precisely that—an intentionally shaped culture—one provides direction to the invention of the mind. (Eisner, 1983, p. 29)

The arts make all kinds of learning exciting. Art making and appreciation serve to uniquely stimulate the senses and provide direct, active pathways to perceptions about the world around us. The arts provide a wealth of experience related to forms of human expression found in language as well as various forms of nonverbal and sensory communication, such as gesture, emotions, feelings, sound, symbols, movement, shapes, colors, patterns, and designs. (Gardner, 1984, 1993a, 1993b). Dance, drama, music, and the visual arts often communicate within nonverbal avenues of expression and use symbols that are simply not translatable to human language. By doing so, they provide important ways of knowing as essential forms of human discourse and inquiry (Eisner, 1980). Human language alone may not provide the sufficient means to communicate many life experiences, emotions, and meanings (California Department of Education, 1996).

As many of us have experienced, children respond actively and joyfully to nonverbal communications and avenues of expression the arts provide. In order to nurture this natural excitement about an important way of learning, all students deserve regular instruction in the arts, an education in the arts that includes doing and making art as well as learning about the arts. This means that children should have frequent and regular opportunities to produce their own works of art; observe artists and performances; examine, discuss, analyze, critique, and compare qualities of art, and by doing so, continue to explore their own and others' cultural heritage and connections to other learning. Furthermore, students should be educated in the arts in order to develop their own artistic skills, knowledge, understanding, and aesthetic values stemming from sequential instruction in the arts (California Department of Education, 1996). Therefore, education in the arts for every child should be a vital component within the larger school curriculum.

If the arts are necessary to preserve and understand culture as well as serve to more fully and humanely educate us about our world, we might need to take a closer look at what the arts teach and if those offerings are appropriate, if not central, to the school curriculum. Within Jensen's definitive compilation of research about the arts and their effect on brain development, *Arts with the Brain in Mind* (2001), the author poses a multi-faceted case for the inclusion of education in the arts within school curriculum. He explains that education in the arts can actively contribute to and enhance learning in other areas of the curriculum as well as provide additional, albeit less measurable, benefits for the development of a child.

Jensen comments on the arts' linkages to other learning by summarizing, "The arts enhance the process of learning. The systems they nourish, which include our integrated sensory, attentional, cognitive, emotional, and motor capactities, are, in fact, the driving forces behind all other learning" (Jensen, 2001, p. 2). In addition to this argument, Jensen provides comments on the extra benefits of arts education by posing the following:

> Why be sheepish about the possibility that the arts may promote self-discipline and motivations? What's embarrassing about countless other art benefits that include aesthetic awareness, cultural exposure, social harmony, creativity, improved emotional expression, and appreciation of diversity? Aren't these the underpinnings of a healthy culture? (p. 3)

Many other considerations and positive changes can be seen in student development when students learn through the arts. The contributors of *Champions of Change: The Impact of the Arts on Learning* (Fiske, 1999) describe the considerable affects of education in the arts:

- Many students who are frequently marginalized or under served (traditionally at-risk student populations or potential dropouts) are motivated through their participation in the arts to alter or eliminate their school absences and tardiness.
- Groups of students who participate in the arts are found to have consistently better communication skills, friendships with others, and fewer instances of violence, racism, and other troubling and nonproductive behaviors.
- Arts disciplines can provide unique learning environments for direct student engagement through personal discovery and group participation. Students can learn to become self-directed learners and willingly experiment with possible solutions to current problems.
- Within these learning environments, students can become challenged to find and value their own level of accomplishment as well as considerable personal satisfaction concerning their contributions to the success of the group. These skills are important to community citizenship, family life, and other important personal relationships as well as toward the preparation of capable working adults who are willing and experienced in working with others to collaboratively create new ideas and successfully solve problems together.

- Students coming from under-served populations gain as much or more from educational experiences in the arts as those coming from areas of higher socioeconomic demographics.

Rather than to be thought of as entertaining or extra-curricular frills, purposeful and valuable education in the arts needs to occur in school settings and within a variety of teaching and learning activities. These activities can be both discipline-specific to the arts as well as integrated or connected to other subject matter learning. These various classroom practices should contribute to the study of, and direct experiences in, the arts as a major teaching discipline area or core subject area of the school curriculum. Important to the purposes of this book, a major discipline is thought of as inclusive, rather than elitist, because it should provide opportunities for the majority, not the few. In other words, an education in the arts should be made available for all children in every school, not just the talented, select few. Furthermore, general education in the arts can be connected to other learning at hand establishing its importance as a valuable way of thinking, learning, doing, and knowing across multiple subject matter.

Murray (1983) stated that the overall goal within such an inclusive general education in the arts is:

> Not to make every student an artist, but to exploit art as a unique vehicle for developing the individual creative potential in every student. As an open-ended, unrestricted context for thinking and caring, art expands our capacity to perceive, understand, and appreciate life. Limited only by the power of our imaginations, art confronts the unknown and attempt the impossible in order to construct new meanings. Art exalts the best and the most that human beings can be; it inspires us to surpass ourselves. (p. 25)

The arts are worthy of study in and of themselves. To this strong argument for the inclusion of arts in education as a core discipline area, Jensen adds, "We should support the arts in education because of their dynamic and broad-based value as a peer of every other widely accepted discipline" (Jensen, 2001, p. 3). Music, dance, drama, and the visual arts are separate disciplines within the larger umbrella concept of all the arts as a unique discipline area, as in education in the arts. Jensen argues that a viable discipline must also contain subdisciplines that add "breadth, depth, and credibility" to that discipline (p. 6). Each of the component arts naturally contain many subdisciplines. In music these areas may include singing, playing of instruments, performance, composing, improvisation, analysis, involvement in the music of many cultures and historical periods, etc. In the visual arts we can add sculpture, drawing, photography, painting, computer-based graphics, fabric design and more. Dance and drama also contain performance, choreography, characterization, improvisation, critique and analysis, costuming, stagecraft and many more components (see table 1.1). Jensen concludes his case for the arts as a viable discipline by offering, "Taken as a whole, the arts are wide ranging and deep in substance" (p. 7).

Learning activities in the arts should include the following opportunities:

- Increasing artistic perception including the processing of information about elements found within the arts
- Creating and performing art
- Analyzing and valuing through learning to make informed judgements about the arts
- Learning about and making connections between the arts within their historical and cultural contexts
- Comparing and connecting learning within the arts with other subject areas

(California Department of Education, 1996; MENC, 1994a).

For the purposes of this chapter, it is helpful to briefly survey overall content standards in each of the four art disciplines: music, dance, theatre (drama), and visual art. To help organize this summary, *The National Standards for Arts Education: What Every Young American Should Know and Be Able to Do in the Arts* (MENC, 1994a) will be directly referenced. This document was selected because it was collaboratively created by prominent arts education representatives from the Consortium of National Arts Education Associations, including the following: American Alliance for Theatre & Education, Music Educators National Conference, National Art Education Association, and the National Dance Association. This broadly ranged, national standard-based, comprehensive guide is one of many documents and guidelines designed to help educators address the need for various forms and components of comprehensive arts education, philosophy and advocacy, specific arts content areas, age- and skill-appropriate teaching goals and objectives, arts teaching content and achievement standards, and resources for teaching.

Table 1.1. Arts Standards

Music Content Standards include:

1. Singing, alone and with others, a varied repertoire of music
2. Performing on instruments, alone and with others, a varied repertoire of music
3. Improvising melodies, variations, and accompaniments
4. Composing and arranging music within specified guidelines
5. Reading and notating music
6. Listening to, analyzing, and describing music
7. Evaluating music and music performances
8. Understanding relationships between music, the other arts, and disciplines outside the arts
9. Understanding music in relation to history and culture

Dance Content Standards include:

1. Identifying and demonstrating movement elements and skills in performing dance
2. Understanding choreographic principles, processes, and structures
3. Understanding dance as a way to create and communicate meaning
4. Applying and demonstrating critical and creative thinking skills in dance
5. Demonstrating and understanding dance in various cultures and historical periods
6. Making connections between dance and healthful living
7. Making connections between dance and other disciplines

In Drama (Theatre), Content Standards include:

1. Script writing by planning and recording improvisations based on personal experience and heritage, imagination, literature, and history
2. Acting by assuming roles and interacting in improvisations
3. Designing by visualizing and arranging environments for classroom dramatizations
4. Directing by planning classroom dramatizations
5. Researching by finding information to support classroom dramatizations
6. Comparing and connecting art forms by describing theatre, dramatic media (such as film, television, and electronic media, and other forms)
7. Analyzing and explaining personal preferences and constructing meanings from classroom dramatizations and from theatre, film, television, and electronic media productions
8. Understanding context by recognizing the role of theatre, film, television, and electronic media in daily life

In Visual Arts, Content Standards include:

1. Understanding and applying media techniques and processes
2. Using knowledge of structures and functions
3. Choosing and evaluating a range of subject matter, symbols, and ideas
4. Understanding the visual arts in relation to history and cultures
5. Reflecting upon and assessing the characteristics of their work and the work of others
6. Making connections between visual arts and other disciplines

In summary, the four arts are a unique and comprehensive discipline area and contain within themselves separate discipline and subdiscipline areas. As part of the core curriculum, an education in the arts is therefore the right of the many, not the few. As such, the arts should be on equal footing within the other subject matter in our classrooms. However, for various reasons, arts specialists might be limited in the amount of children they can teach.

The responsibility to teach the arts to all our children could lie with classroom teachers at the elementary and middle school level because most school sites do not offer specialist instruction in all four arts areas for all children. Classroom teachers are often responsible for multiple subject matter, therefore practical ways of purposefully integrating the arts within other classroom learning are both necessary and appropriate for these ends (see chapter 2). Finally, it should be our goal as educators to promote the presence of quality arts education as a valued and much-beloved part of our daily teaching environments in as many classrooms as possible. If these challenges ring true, who then will teach the children about the arts? How can this be done?

Questions for further discussion, study, and project development:

- What are the four arts? Name the subdisciplines within each of the arts.
- What are the benefits of instruction in the arts?
- How are the arts a discipline/core subject area?
- What knowledge and skills must a person have to do or make art?
- What must a person know to appreciate a product of the arts (concert, dance, play, museum display, etc.)?
- Is direct experience in the arts essential to understanding various forms of art? Why or why not?

CHAPTER 2

What Is Arts Integration?

The world of reality has its limits; the world of imagination is boundless.

—Jean-Jacques Rousseau

"Beauty is of value only when recreated by those who discover it. . . . The goal in education is not to increase the amount of knowledge, but to create possibilities for a child to invent and discover."
—Jean Piaget

If we know that an education in the arts is crucial to a child's development and understanding of the world, our overriding goal should be to educate all of our children in the arts. Chapter 1 covered the distinct bodies of knowledge imbedded within the arts disciplines, as well as how that knowledge base actively contributes to other forms of learning. It is important that the national standards in each of the four arts clearly articulate that education in the arts can and should regularly establish natural and purposeful linkages to disciplines outside the arts, an understanding of the arts in relationship to contexts of history and culture, and the role of the arts within daily life (MENC, 1994a). But who can provide this kind of broad-based arts education to all children?

Many children are taught by arts specialists, usually in music and visual art only. Because all children do not have exposure to an education in all four arts areas, there is a need to rethink our possibilities for delivering these content areas to more children. Our experience suggests that this goal can be accomplished within purposeful integrated contexts, where children's learning in the arts is vitally connected to other learning at hand, without sacrificing the integrity or worth of the arts as distinct discipline content areas. With these perceptions in mind, how do we best provide an education in the arts linked to other classroom learning?

Herein lies a substantial basis of inquiry for this chapter to address: What are some advantages and disadvantages of teaching in a discipline-specific specialized manner and are there other ways to teach the arts? What does it mean to integrate or teach in an interdisciplinary manner and what are some types, forms, and examples of curriculum integration using the arts? What are the advantages of integrating the arts into language arts and other subject areas? What are some pitfalls of integration? Who should teach integrated arts within the schools? What are some goals to reach, as well as obstacles to achieving them? How can we begin? Finally, for purposes of clarity and application, an active teaching model of an integrated arts lesson correlated to ideas within this chapter is offered.

What Are Some Advantages and Disadvantages to Teaching in a Discipline-Specific Manner and Are There Other Ways to Teach the Arts?

Within many schools, teachers and students become used to separating learning within certain subjects or specific activity time periods. Jacobs (1989), in her definitive work, *Interdisciplinary Curriculum: Design and Implementation*, writes about a second grader who describes mathematics as "something you do in the morning." It could be true that this rather amusing antidote hints at a more serious, composite portrait of our students' daily instructional lives within multiple compartmentalized and separated learning experiences at school. Jacobs contends that as children mature, they "complain that school is irrelevant to the larger world. In the real world, we do not wake up in the morning and do social studies for fifty minutes . . . in real life, we encounter problems and situations, gather data from all of our resources, and generate solutions. The fragmented school day does not reflect this reality" (p. 1). Students and teachers might feel disconnected from a more holistic view of the learning that goes on within the school environment and that learning in school is somehow irrelevant to students' lives and their growing knowledge of the world around them.

However, we all know that in order for children to learn to read well, write or do math, understand science and social studies, proper instructional time must be allotted for these learnings on a regular basis. The arts also require attention and deserve time. Teacher expertise, space, materials, resources, and best practices must exist for students to correctly master learning within each of these content area disciplines. The point here is not to suggest that schools should not have discipline-based instruction, but rather that something else might also be needed.

Other kinds of instruction are equally valuable and can indeed serve to augment and enhance discipline-based instruction. Jacobs suggests that in addition to discipline-based instruction schools "also need to create learning experiences that periodically demonstrate the relationship of the disciplines, thus heightening their relevancy. There is a need to actively show students how different subject areas influence their lives, and it is critical that students see the strength of each discipline perspective in a connected way" (p. 5). Therefore, one goal for student learning may include connection and synthesis, not isolation and compartmentalization, of separate knowledge bases.

What Does It Mean to Integrate or Teach in an Interdisciplinary Manner and What Are Some Forms and Examples of Curriculum Integration Using the Arts?

In addition to engaging children within specific learning perimeters defined by various arts content standards, teachers can choose to design interdisciplinary curriculum in which students experience deeper understanding of the arts through "the intersections and interactions of the disciplines" (Barrett, 2001, p. 27). In this context, the arts are integrated with each other and with other subject areas as an active way to enhance overall instruction, not to compete or replace discipline specific teaching and learning. In her work concerning the meaningful integration of the arts with other disciplines, Snyder (2001) suggests that there are three meaningful ways to link disciplines or intelligences to enhance student learning including the following:

- **Connection: One discipline in the service of another** An example might be when a teacher uses material or activity from another discipline or disciplines (i.e., poetry writing/language arts) to reinforce a concept or skill learning within another (i.e., setting poetry to melody/music) or the use of components of a visual art work (featuring elements of repetition, contrast, form, etc.) to help teach the same concepts in dance, drama, music, mathematics, science, or another discipline. These connections can be between arts or arts connected to another subject matter. The goal here is to enhance learning within the subject matter at hand by drawing from and connecting to learning within another subject area.

- *Correlation: Two disciplines share common materials or activities* An example of correlation includes the intersection or common conceptual grounding of two discipline-specific concepts or skills, such as math activities involving fractions and proportions of the whole, which become instructionally correlated with concepts of whole, half, quarter, etc. in musical note values and notation. Another example of correlation might be activity using a historical time line of events in American history (social studies) linked or correlated to how those events shaped certain lyrics of songs sung during that time (music and language arts).

- *Integration: Each discipline addresses the chosen theme from its unique perspective* A broad theme is chosen so that it can cut across multiple discipline areas, allowing students to use their learning within content areas to explore the theme in meaningful and valid ways. *Topical* instructional themes can include such things as animal life, stars, rain forests, rivers of the world, colors, historical events, specific holidays, cultures, etc. *Conceptual* themes can include ideas involving broader, more comprehensive instructional themes, such as patterns, the universe, music of many cultures, structures (manmade and natural), environments, imagination, famous speeches, highlights of the twentieth century, peace, heroes, courage, respect, tolerance, etc. Both topical and conceptual themes can be used within grade-specific contexts (linked to specific curricular themes) as well as within broader, across-the-grades, school-wide contexts.

Barrett, McCoy, and Veblen (1997) further articulate ways to integrate using actual works of art. These works of art may be listened to, watched, performed, or viewed and can include an actual piece of music, a dance, a play or scene, a painting, a piece of children's literature, a poem, etc. These works of art then become instructional centerpieces for valid connections to other subject areas. According to Barrett, these kinds of connections can serve to both preserve the integrity of the arts content as well as establish validity through purposeful and meaningful connection. In her work concerning works of music and their role in integrated teaching, Barrett (2001) offers, "When connections between music and another discipline are valid, the bonds between the disciplines are organic; that is, they make sense without forcing a fit or stretching a point. Valid connections carry meaning across the boundaries of subject areas" (p. 28). This kind of "arts work" integration focuses on the following questions for teacher and student inquiry that can naturally and purposefully serve to connect interdisciplinary subject matter:

> Who created the work of art? When and where was it created? Why and for whom was it created? What is its subject? What is being expressed? What techniques did its creator use to help us understand what is being expressed? What kind of structure or form does it have? What does it sound or look like? (Barrett, McCoy, and Veblen, 1997, p. 77)

Specific examples of this kind of interdisciplinary connection include a high school assignment involving the study of American hymns and shape note singing styles and their connection to the "character of musical life in the colonial and Revolutionary War periods" (p. 29). This integrative study included listening activity to authentic examples of this period of American music, active experimentation with various kinds of vocal production associated with this type of singing, and finally, a performance of works. Another of Barrett's examples involves lower grade instruction in which classroom teachers and arts specialists collaborate in integrative instruction featuring a wordless children's book, *I See a Song*, by Eric Carle (1973). This collaboration was designed to emphasize the "expressive dimensions of children's literature" (p. 30). Carle's book became a catalyst for students' creative response activity that Barrett elaborates in the following way:

> First, the teachers encourage children to think about the maestro's preface on the (book's) title page, "I see a song; I paint music; I hear color," by asking them "What does this mean? How do these illustrations fit with the maestro's curious statements? Can you see a song, paint music, and hear color?" The classroom teacher helps one group of children to write a poem using figures of speech and vivid adjectives and adverbs to portray the gradual infusion of color. The art specialist guides an exploration of color value and hue with another group of students as they layer colored tissue paper to construct a collage of thickening texture using a technique similar to Carle's. The music specialist works with a composition group to compose a musical score using recorders, xylophones, and small percussion instruments. Students select timbres and layer motives to create the same sense of unfolding excitement that Carle produces

with color, line, and shape. The children then come together to present their ideas and to experience the vibrant interplay of materials, moods, and ideas. One student suggests using movement to tie the students' poem, collage, and instrumental composition together, and the group decides to continue exploring these interesting possibilities. (Barrett, 2001, p. 30)

What Are the Advantages of Integrating the Arts into Language Arts and Other Subject Areas?

Vygotsky (1978) argued that human language is developed through multiple signs, both verbal and nonverbal, during which learners connect learning to what they already know. Synthesis takes place through a child's active involvement with the meanings of language. Furthermore, we know the centrality of human language toward thinking and that a child's learning depends on language, cutting across learning within all subject matter and school activity.

Integrative activities in which the arts' verbal and nonverbal communications and systems of thought are actively and creatively connected to learning within reading, writing, and oral language development can serve to heighten student interest and expressive involvement with learning at hand. By doing so, the arts are naturally connected to many subject areas. Purposeful integrated arts teaching contains many active avenues toward the literacy development of young readers (Hancock, 2000). By doing so, the arts can lend important experiences and context for language development. Ogle (1986) summarizes:

Therefore, if we want learners to construct more relationships across ideas and synthesize these in ways that promote higher order thinking, then those adults responsible for teaching children need to implement language and sign systems that foster connections and help students understand the similarities and differences across disciplinary boundaries . . . . These ways of interaction are not formed in isolation, but are, instead, more integrative of multiple aspects of knowledge. (Ogle, 1986, p. 4)

Through various kinds of planned, purposeful integrative activities, students can directly and actively experience natural, unforced, authentic, and valid connections between the arts and other disciplines that are designed to enhance and augment students' understanding through meaningful learning activity.

What Are Some Pitfalls of Integration?

This chapter has offered considerations and ways to purposefully and effectively integrate subject matter. However, be aware of possible pitfalls some busy teachers face as they plan and select materials and activities for integrated teaching that might not result in authentic, valid, and meaningful experiences for increased student learning. When mistakes occur, they usually include the following characteristics: lack of clear planning and instructional purpose, lack of informed background information, lack of planning and collaboration between teachers and discipline knowledge bases, limited scope concerning quality sources, and/or (where appropriate resources are found) potpourri effect or fragmented curriculum connections, forced or artificial connections, and the watering down of content in the disciplines involved.

An example of some of these pitfalls can be best illustrated by this veteran classroom teacher's reflection:

> I tried to connect my social studies unit on the California Gold Rush to pioneer songs, diaries of real people of the time, folk dances, and paintings of the period. I don't have much planning time, as usual, so I just looked in our state music and art texts and hoped the paintings and a song recorded on the CD provided would help me quickly teach an integrated Gold Rush lesson on our one free afternoon. However, none of the songs talked about mining for gold, so I trashed the whole idea and hurriedly thought of another idea for our grade-level assembly the next day. I decided instead to create papier-mache gold-mining bowls. I wish I could have established better connections, but I just couldn't.

Who Should Teach Integrated Arts within the Schools?

Because the arts are core curriculum, the responsibility to educate all our children in the arts falls to every teacher in the school. Learning occurs with and through the arts. Naturally, K–8 arts specialists can provide students with a depth of knowledge in specific disciplines, particularly and most frequently in music and visual art. However, many arts specialists have had programs eliminated or systematically marginalized, and might not be able to offer more than one instruction per week in their art area (usually music and visual art only). Furthermore, some arts specialists teach a small percentage of the school population, or those students who have elected to take art, instrumental music, drama, and other school arts classes. Compounding these problems, music specialists, for instance, often teach within overloaded schedules, itinerant teaching assignments, large classes, and performance responsibilities that can negatively affect their opportunities to interface with other teachers and the curricular needs of all the students within the larger school environment (McDonald, 2000).

Additionally, dance and drama specialists are uncommon or nonexistent within many elementary and middle school sites. Therefore, instruction in these two arts specialty areas often falls to teachers of language arts, English, and P.E., or those teachers who have special interest in exposing these arts to children. Furthermore, the arts specialists' isolation from other teachers at the school sites is sometimes interpreted by others as disinterest in classroom teachers' instructional needs linked to student learning in other content areas. Consequently, specialized instruction in the arts can sometimes be thought of as disconnected from teaching and learning in other school subjects (see chapter 7). If arts specialists are limited in their ability to teach all the children about the arts, to whom can we turn? The classroom teacher?

Several concerns impact the delivery of arts education to all children in our elementary and middle school general classrooms. First, in light of current emphasis on standards-based testing, assessment, and teacher accountability, many classroom educators feel hesitant about exploring teaching strategies designed to integrate the arts into their existing classroom curriculum. Within these circumstances, the purpose and need to actively include the arts within classroom teaching might be unclear. Although we know the arts, too, have clearly articulated standards and perimeters toward assessment and are indeed core curriculum, they are not currently assessed with the same prioritized rigor and seriousness as other content areas. Therefore, many educators assume that arts instruction should not and cannot be given the same kind of time, resources, instructional focus, and professional growth emphasis as other core content areas in the general classroom. Classroom teachers might be limited in their own content background in the arts and/or lack encouragement, teaching strategies and models, materials, resources, and professional development concerning how to infuse or integrate the arts within the general curriculum. What is the answer to the question, "Who will teach in an integrated manner?"

For change to occur, we need: time, structured curriculum planning and teaching collaborations between classroom teachers and arts specialists, developmentally appropriate understanding and skills in arts curricula tied to other subject matter, open-mindedness toward problem-solving, long-range goals, professional development in integration, inclusion of parent, student, community input and resources, humor, teacher reflection, and ways to evaluate and access integrated teaching and learning (Snyder, 2001). However, we know changes in how we teach can indeed have their roots in one person's ideas, which then, through example, begin to lead others.

With careful planning and purposeful collaboration, successful integrated curriculum can be initiated by two teachers who desire to work together, even if others are not interested. As time, experimentation, evaluation, and reflection evolve out of integrated experiences, other teachers can be brought into the group. As Snyder (2001) suggests, "Each teacher and school will necessarily adapt interdisciplinary techniques to individual needs, and new research being done on curricular integration will help inform decisions. There will be programs specific to a school, a grade level, a discipline, a district, a university course, or a statewide initiative" (p. 38).

What Are Some Obstacles to Achieving Goals in Integrated Teaching?

Do we have the courage to create integrated curricula? We know we will have to explore new teaching and learning territory and be willing to experiment across grade levels, disciplines, and classrooms. In order to begin to shape effective instruction, we will need to seek administrative support and commitment to the need for professional growth, planning time, and collaboration with our peers.

This chapter has offered definitions, purposes, and examples of integration in which the arts can be used to increase student learning to, with, and across many disciplines. The following teaching model further illustrates this chapter's content and provides a tangible integrated example toward discussion and curriculum planning.

ACTIVE INTEGRATION TEACHING MODEL

Expressive literacy within musical listening: *The Moldau,* a symphonic poem by Smetana

Introduction

Within class, teachers are encouraged to infuse literacy activities into all music and integrated arts experiences. Young students are consistently encouraged to read aloud and evocatively respond to song texts and listening activities through movement, visual art, drama, and creative writing. Integrated lesson models become a purposeful set of activities designed to increase the child's learning through active involvement in expressive oral language (Cox, 1998; Jacobs, 1989, 1997; Lapp and Flood 1992; McDonald and Fisher, 1999b; Rosenblatt, 1978; Vygotsky, 1962, 1978). Song texts, for example, are poetry embedded within melodic and rhythmic settings. Their poetic contexts can include rich historical and cultural frameworks or dramatic settings of potential interest to young children, if taught actively and expressively (Cohn, 1993; Tarlow, 1998; Levene, 1993).

A purposeful and well-prepared musical listening activity in which song texts are read aloud could be considered active uses of expressive literacy. Such activities may also contain potential curricular extensions through their natural connections to social studies, math, and science contexts—connections so needed by classroom teachers who might have limited background and time, but great interest, in the teaching of the music and other arts (Barry, 1998).

New Territory for Expressive Literacy: Symphonic Poems

Potential curriculum material for expressive literacy activities might be found within perceived "forbidden" musical territory to the nonspecialist—that of the great symphonic literature of the late nineteenth century! Many orchestral masterpieces of this Romantic period in Western classical music are programmed compositions, *symphonic poems,* in which major sections of the music are thematically tied to the composer's intended "plot" or sequence of musical metaphor. Composer Franz Liszt, a prolific writer of this genre, composed thirteen symphonic poems between 1848 and 1882. Liszt's format included relatively short pieces that were not partitioned into separate movements, but rather in:

> a continuous form with various sections more or less contrasting in character and tempo . . . *Poem* in this designation may refer simply to the root meaning of the word—something "made," invented—or perhaps to the poetic content in the sense of the program of each work . . . suggested by some picture, statue, drama, poem, scene, personality, thought, impression, or other object not identifiable from the music alone. It is, however, identified by the composer's title and usually also by a prefatory note. (Grout, 1973, p. 586)

The great Czech composer Bedrich Smetana (1824–1884) wrote a piece entitled *Ma Vlast* (My Fatherland), a nationalistic musical composition about his homeland. As in much Romantic literature, art, and poetry of this period of European history, musical subjects interpreted intense patriotism, aesthetic responses to naturalistic settings, romantic longings, and idolized or heroic settings. Within Smetana's work, *Ma Vlast*, is an eleven-minute symphonic poem entitled, *The Moldau*, named after the great Czech river. The Moldau flows from its origins in the Alps, through the countryside to the capital city of Prague, and eventually to the sea. The music captures the imaginary experience of floating on the river and experiencing the sights, sounds, and feelings of its changing landscapes and forms.

Smetana wrote references to the images he wished to illuminate through his music in *The Moldau*. It is from the composer's original descriptive program notes that I constructed the following expressive literacy/guided musical listening and visual art activity for third-through eighth-grade students. The activity is structured to present the written and then orally interpreted poetic images Smetana desired his audience to know before listening to his musical composition. It has been my considerable experience that preliminary visual and aural focus on the symphonic poem's story line allows the student listener to be guided through the orchestral piece, thereby increasing involvement with and enjoyment of the listening experience.

Strategies and Activities for Listening to *The Moldau*

Pre-set/Expressive Speech

Before playing the musical recording of *The Moldau*, the teacher could read aloud each of the symphonic poem cards (see the following list). The teacher's expressive oral model could then be echoed by the students card by card. Share with the students the desire to have the words read in group "unison" style, everyone staying together as in a dramatic choral reading. Suggest that students read as "actors attempting to set the scene" for a musical journey. Students can be encouraged to create beauty with their words—words that paint pictures during the musical listening, just as Smetana intended in his symphonic poem.

Students are asked to read the title and composer's name (card #1). Share with the students Smetana's desire to capture the sights, sounds, and people of his beloved homeland by having his audience read the symphonic poem in the program before the music is performed. It is important that no other visuals are shown other than the following text cards.

Symphonic Poem Cards

Each line may be written on large posters or overheads and recited slowly in this order:

1. *The Moldau*, a symphonic poem by Smetana

    - Deep in the mountain forest . . . the little stream comes to life . . .
    - bubbling, churning . . .
    - swirling, splashing over rocks and boulders . . .
    - cascading over waterfalls . . .
    - through the woods . . . the sounds of hunters on horseback . . .
    - around the bend . . . a village wedding and its colorful peasant dancers
    - moonlight—silver swirls . . . deep purple silent water . . .
    - building, churning into three giant waterfalls . . .
    - past the walls of the great castle of Prague . . .
    - the final journey . . .
    - the great river Moldau flows boldly to the sea.
    - The End.

Listening Activity/Visual Art with Text Cues to the Music

Arrange the posters or overheads in their original text order.

Ask the students to get their drawing paper, crayons, or pastels. Invite the students to sit quietly in order to maintain aural focus and prepare for a guided listening experience. Ask the students to write the name of the composition and the composer on the top of their art paper. Tell the students:

We are ready to listen, but we are about to listen with our ears and eyes! Smetana described his countryside through his music. We have his words about the journey of the Moldau, and his ideas through his music. As the music plays, I would like you to illustrate how you see the music. You may sketch the entire piece or just a particular scene that you like. I will hold up the card of the section of the music we are "in" as it is playing. You need to look up from your artwork whenever you think we might be in a new section in the music. I will help you by softly snapping my fingers and holding up the new card. Okay, let's announce our piece, (together, out loud for focus) "*The Moldau*, a symphonic poem by Smetana."

The recording (eleven minutes in length) is played as the students quietly illustrate. During the listening/visual art activity, the teacher can hold up the appropriate card sections. Note: Teachers can best prepare this lesson by listening to *The Moldau* several times in order to distinguish text sections in the music. This is easily done. It is also helpful to avoid giving oral instruction over the sound of the recorded music because the students are participating in a listening activity with focus on the musical references to the symphonic poem sequence they have just read aloud.

It might be effective to hang the posters in reading sequence on a clothes line (with clothespins) so that the readers can see where they are in the thematic material and what is about to happen in the music. The teacher can simply silently stand behind the card and physically indicate where they are in the musical sequence.

Lesson Extensions

After the recording is played, ask the students to hold up or display their artwork. Tell the students to look around the room at all the interpretations of Smetena's symphonic poem. Invite dialogue about as many student art pieces as possible and display them within a created composers' bulletin board (complete with fine art of the historical period) or within students' illustrated journals (portfolios). Portfolios could also include responses to other musical compositions, poetry, or fine art from many cultural styles, origins, genres, and time periods.

Upper elementary students can be encouraged to design a large poster mural depicting oversized scenes of *The Moldau* themes. As the recording is played, the students slowly unroll the mural and then physically dramatize a small, no dialogue, movement scene in front of the background as the music continues playing. *The Moldau*'s scene of "colorful peasant dancers" lends itself particularly well to students' creative movement and folkdance interpretations because the music of this section is a Czech folk dance melody. Consult the basal text series in elementary music (i.e., Silver Burdett and Ginn *The Music Connection* © 1995 or *Making Music* © 2002) for music and dance instructions of Czech and/or other Eastern European folk dances.

Older children might enjoy the experience of "teaching" the Moldau activity to a younger group of children at their school setting. Allow these students to research all they can about Smetana, the Czech Republic, the Moldau, Prague, and Romantic period visual art, and infuse those resources into the lessons they teach to other students.

Use the curricular theme of water cycles to explore children's literature and poetry about the great rivers of the United States and other countries: Amazon, Mississippi, Nile, Yellow River, Danube, Columbia, Colorado, Seine, Ganges, etc. Find indigenous music, literature, poetry, and visual art to surround these themes and resulting activities for extensions to social studies, reading, poetry, science, and math.

Commentary

A fifth grader shared the following:

> Now, when I read books and poems and stuff about rivers, I think about *The Moldau*. Sometimes I can hear some of the music and pretend I'm on that river. I wish all the rivers had some music to go with them so I could pretend I was traveling on them.

During *The Moldau* lesson debriefing, one elementary teacher commented:

> This was an incredibly therapeutic lesson for me! I feel calm and focused and, for the first time, I was able to listen to a classical piece and not be overwhelmed by it. I usually get lost and frustrated within that wall of musical sound! I feel I could definitely use this idea and could enjoy teaching great music in this way. Thanks! We need more connections like this!

In a similar way, a fourth grader exclaimed:

> Can we hear that again? Let's close our eyes and then see if we know where we are in the music and then open them, look at the cards, and check. I'm going to tell my grandma to get that *Moldau* thing for me for Christmas!

Traditional musical listening activities are powerful and evocative within their own right—however, musical listening combined with lessons utilizing expressive literacy could serve to enhance the students' ability to focus and understand both the music as well as the written thematic material. If students feel a part of the musical composition—that is, intimately involved in the self-constructed meanings of the sound experience, they may be empowered to experience a rarity in many classroom settings—immersion into beauty, the aesthetic foundation of all art.

Questions for further discussion, study, and project development:

- What does it mean to integrate or teach in an interdisciplinary manner?
- Explain connection, correlation, and integration. What are some examples of each of these tied to your own classroom curricula?
- What are some advantages of arts integration within other curricula?
- What are some hazards or pitfalls of curriculum integration? Using this chapter's Gold Rush example, what are some of the teacher's mistakes and what might she do instead to establish purposeful integration?
- Who could teach integrated arts in the schools?
- What are some goals to reach?

CHAPTER 3

How Can the Arts Be Infused into Reading and Language Arts Instruction in My Classroom?

Trust that still, small voice that says, "This might work and I'll try it."

—Diane Mariechild

The previous two chapters covered why and how we might integrate instruction toward the development of arts-loving readers. This chapter offers insights into the use of integrated arts within reading and language arts instruction.

Across the world, teachers are working to improve the literacy performance of their students. Many teachers have created and implemented innovative approaches to translate current research into classroom practices. Given the explosion of information available concerning literacy development, teachers are considering new approaches to their instructional repertoires. For example, we know that a young child's developing literacy skills are exercised when "emergent readers hear, sing, discuss, play with, and write songs, they are building important background knowledge that they will draw upon during later reading and writing experiences. With each new song, students learn concepts and word meanings that they will encounter in print" (Smith, 2000, p. 647).

This chapter begins with information about the instructional approaches that teachers use to provide literacy instruction, including read-aloud, shared reading, guided reading, independent reading, and writing. Other chapters explore additional instructional strategies, such as readers' theater (see chapter 5) and performances as a way of learning (see chapter 4). Following the instructional strategies, we provide specific examples of the use of the arts within emergent literacy instruction, including the use of drawing, music and movement, singing, creative movement, and creative drama. This section focuses on concepts of print, the sense of story and sequence, phonemic awareness and phonics, background knowledge and vocabulary, and basic spelling patterns. Additional integrated arts education and language arts lessons for older students are in chapters 4 and 5.

READ-ALOUDS

Many very young children beg their parents and the other important adults in their lives to read stories to them. It is enjoyable to both the adult and the child; through this warm and pleasant activity, many children develop a love of books. Reading stories to children in the classroom is one way teachers can attempt to replicate the treasured activity of lap reading experienced by many children at home (Frey, Fisher, Lapp, and Flood, 1999). Those children unfortunate enough not to have had numerous lap-reading experiences have a desperate need for the teacher to welcome them to the world of literature and to experience reading in this manner. By reading aloud, the teacher models reading behavior; students see that reading is a pleasurable experience, a way to learn, and something to be shared with others. During read-alouds, teachers have the added opportunity to model expressive speech and characterization so vital in understanding and doing drama. Listening to books being read aloud is also a way for students to experience those books that are too difficult for them to read themselves or that are of a genre they themselves would not have chosen. Teachers of every grade should read to their students every day of the school year.

In primary grade classrooms, read-aloud time is frequently scheduled during the morning literacy block or immediately following lunch. If a regular time is reserved for reading aloud, students expect and anticipate the activity. In upper grade and middle school classrooms, teachers typically reserve a specific time each day for read-alouds. Thus, students come to expect their teacher to read to them and anticipate the event with excitement.

Teachers should select books appropriate for the interests and needs of their students. Young children enjoy picture books with predictable story lines and repetitious texts. Students quickly learn repeated phrases and join in with the teacher as they are read. Intermediate-grade teachers can allow students to select books to be read aloud. However, it is important, particularly in the primary grades, that all books read be examples of well-written literature that can include well-constructed and engaging visual art. Books read by the teacher are perceived by students as those worthy of the teacher's time and attention; therefore, they set the standard for the types of books the students will choose for independent reading. We suggest that teachers choose texts with:

1. literary quality that has been demonstrated by reviews, awards, and trusted word-of-mouth recommendations.
2. aesthetic qualities that cover a wide array of genres (e.g., historical fiction, mystery, fantasy, biography, poetry, etc.) that will elicit thoughtful responses from children.
3. authentic representations of characters, settings, times, and historical events, as appropriate for the genre.
4. text structures that allow for teaching points.
5. concepts and ideas that children can grasp with guidance, not texts that are exceedingly difficult or far below the students' interest level.
6. opportunities to lead children to make unique discoveries about their world.

Teachers can follow a few simple guidelines to make the most of the experience. Children should be seated comfortably on the floor or on small chairs in a semicircle around the teacher, who is also seated on the floor or on a low chair. The book should be held so that the illustrations are visible to all children. By pausing after each page is read, the teacher provides the students with time to view the illustrations in detail and to offer relevant comments or ask questions about the story. In this way, the book's artwork can enhance the children's comprehension and meaningful interaction with the text. The teacher could also pause periodically, at appropriate times, to ask students to make predictions about the story. The sensitive teacher allows students to determine the pace of the read-aloud session and responds to their need to stop and discuss the story in an unhurried manner. Time may also be allotted for discussion following a reading. Arts activities related to the story (e.g., singing a song, pantomiming a scene; illustrating the beginning, middle, and end) are often done following the read-aloud. Response activities are wonderful, but should not be used to excess; sometimes it's desirable just to hear a good story. When reading books that take several days to complete, the teacher should read ahead and identify appropriate stopping places as well as opportunities to feature musical listening and discussion, dramatic interpretations, visualization and responses to art, and creative movement activities. These connections should not be artificial, distracting, or forced. Rather, these connections should be purposeful and facilitate comprehension of the text.

It is important, particularly in the primary grades, for books that are read aloud by the teacher to be placed in the classroom library. Martinez and Teale (1988) found that kindergarten students chose familiar books from the classroom library more frequently than unfamiliar books and they displayed more reading behaviors when looking at books that were familiar to them. This study also confirmed the importance of selecting books with predictable structures; emergent reading behaviors were more evident with books that had predictable story structures.

It cannot be overemphasized that reading aloud should not be an activity exclusive to the primary grades. All students enjoy and benefit from the experience of being read to (Richardson, 2000). For example, a middle school social studies teacher began her lesson on the Holocaust by reading the book *The Butterfly* (Polacco, 2000). Following her read aloud, she invited students to illustrate their reactions to the book and write a sentence or two in response to their created illustrations. She also played music from the time period (French and Jewish folk music) in the background as students illustrated. This opening event provided students with some background information about the unit of study, created an artistic environment for comprehending the text, and sparked some questions that motivated them to learn more.

SHARED READING

Shared reading is a variation of read-alouds—the book is read aloud. Many of the same recommendations found in the read-aloud section apply to shared reading. The difference between read-alouds and shared reading is that shared reading requires that the students all see the text as the teacher reads. Many primary grade teachers do this with big books. Upper grade teachers sometimes photocopy their reading material, use an overhead projector, or obtain copies for each student. As with read-alouds, in shared reading lessons the selection of texts is crucial. For shared reading, we suggest that the teacher purposefully select a text and identify a specific teaching point. For example, *Wings* by James Marshall is a tale of two chickens. One enjoys reading and the other does not. The one who doesn't like reading is captured by a fox. This text could be used for shared reading with any one of the following lessons in mind:

- Focus on how the author uses punctuation — . , ! ? " are all used.
- Focus on dialogue and how authors indicate that characters are talking.
- Focus on specific spelling patterns.

In a second grade classroom, the teacher decided to focus on the use of punctuation during his shared reading of *Wings*. This focus allowed the teacher to use his voice to demonstrate the ways readers should read punctuation and how he changes his voice when different characters are talking. This technique is a natural connection to the skills children need to read dramatic dialogue and performances.

Shared reading lessons often last between fifteen and twenty minutes. Intermediate level teachers usually do not read the entire text as a shared reading—they select the part of the text that contains the information for the lesson that day and then finish the text as a read-aloud or invite students to read the remainder of the text independently or with partners. Remember, shared reading should allow students to see a clear connection between the text that is read to them and some aspect of text structure that is taught.

Again, text selection is very important in shared reading. The text should be engaging and interesting for students. It should also allow the teacher to provide a specific lesson about the text structure. Fortunately, many good books do this. Chapter 6 provides a list of books about the arts and artists. Many of these books are especially good choices for shared reading because they use specific vocabulary that can become the focus of a shared reading lesson with natural and purposeful linkages to teaching content within the arts.

GUIDED READING

Guided reading is the time each day that teachers meet with small groups of students for specific instruction in reading. The students in these groups are often selected because they have similar skills and needs in their reading development. Groups typically consist of between three and five students. Entire books have been written about guided reading instruction (e.g., Fountas and Pinnell, 1996). Essentially, guided reading allows teachers to provide students with new strategies that they can use while reading. As Fountas and Pinnell note, "The idea is for children to take on novel texts, read them at once with a minimum of support, and read many of them again and again for independence and fluency" (p. 2). After the students have read the text and the teacher has provided instruction, the group discusses the story. The teacher then extends the discussion into activities including drama, writing, art, or additional reading on the topic. Each of these extensions or follow-up activities allows the teacher an opportunity to use the arts in the classroom.

It is important that a teacher select an appropriate text to ensure the success of a guided reading lesson. Again, chapter 6 provides a list of resources about arts and artists. Chapter 4 contains lists of poems that can be used during guided reading. In addition to text selection, the prompts a teacher uses are crucial. For example, while students were reading *What a Wonderful World* (Weiss and Thiele, 1995), the teacher asked one student "Did you have enough words to match as you read it with your finger?" This same teacher suggested to another student "Try that again and think about what would make sense with the picture." To another student, the teacher said, "you made one mistake, can you find it?" Although these prompts seem simple, the teacher knew enough about each student and the text to provide support for their reading, yet challenge them to develop skills. At the end of the guided reading session, the teacher provided students with a cassette tape version of the recording of "What a Wonderful World" by Louis Armstrong to listen to during their independent reading time while following along with the book.

WRITING

Writing activities cannot be separated from reading activities, because writing instruction is a necessary companion to reading instruction (Dahl and Farnan, 1998). To become literate, children need systematic instruction in both reading and writing. Early writing instruction should focus on mastering conventions (grammar, punctuation, capitalization, etc.) not merely studying and memorizing them, but really conquering conventions to effectively communicate a message (Fearn and Farnan, 1998).

In a number of ways, teachers integrate arts to contribute to early writing instruction for students. For example, a teacher used the chant, "Miss White Had Fright." After the children were able to clap and speak the chant together, the teacher asked students to write replacement lines for the third line of the chant. The following sentence frames were provided for the children to write a new text line for the chant; "Saw a _____ on a _____" or "Saw a _____ in a _____" or "Saw a _____ with a _____." The children then performed their new chants adding their own ideas and creative movements. To add a visual arts extension to this delightful writing activity, the teacher asked the children to write out and illustrate their new verses for a class book entitled *Miss White's Frightful Night.*

Another way that teachers encourage early writing is to play music and invite students to illustrate what they hear. For example, a second grade teacher recently played the song "In Las Pulgas de San Jose" to her class. While they listened to the song, they sketched on large pieces of paper. When the song finished, the students immediately began writing about their illustrations. These sketches were later used as scenery and props in singing and dramatic performances of the song text. Clearly, the music allowed these students to focus on their thoughts and reduced the procrastination time often associated with writing prompts.

Additional arts-related prompts have been used by teachers. A fourth grade teacher used a digital photo that she had taken. She shared this with students using an LCD projector. The students were encouraged to look at the photo for sixty seconds, writing down single words that came to mind. When the minute was up, the teacher asked students to write about the photo using the words that they had recorded. The students noticed foreground, background, color, season, lighting—all of which are related to understanding and appreciating components of visual art.

Another teacher used wordless books to encourage students to write. A number of wordless books are available that older students find interesting. For example, *Time Flies* (Rohmann, 1994) starts in a museum and without words tells the story of the time of the dinosaurs. Two additional visual arts-related wordless books are *You Can't Take a Balloon into the Metropolitan Museum* (Weitzman and Glasser, 1998) and *You Can't Take a Balloon into the National Gallery* (Weitzman and Glasser, 2000). Both of these books provide wonderful pictures, reproductions, and original art for students to write about. As a side benefit, they also introduce students to museums and the expected behavior inside museums.

FOCUSING ON EMERGENT LITERACY

After covering some of the general instructional strategies that teachers use during reading and language arts time and how the arts can be integrated, we turn our focus to early literacy instruction. Emergent literacy is crucial for students to become lifelong readers and writers. The teachers' focus on early literacy allows students to break the code and read real words. This, in turn, allows students to read fluently and comprehend what they read. In other words, the instruction that young or struggling students receive as their understanding of print emerges is crucial. We focus on five areas of emergent literacy, including concepts of print, a sense of story and sequence, phonemic awareness and phonics, background knowledge and vocabulary, and basic spelling patterns.

CONCEPTS OF PRINT

One of the early predictors of reading success for young children is their understanding of the ways in which print functions. This construct, known as "concepts of print" (e.g., Clay, 1985) includes the knowledge that print, not pictures, contains the message, how to hold a book, the difference between upper- and lowercase letters, left-to-right print orientation, top-to-bottom directionality, and the use of punctuation marks.

Musical activity is an excellent way to explore concepts of print. For example, when teachers use published music big books (large chart paper with chants or poetry written on them), they physically point to and model the left-to-right, top-to-bottom orientation and directionality that characterizes the English language. Similarly, as music teachers encourage students to follow along with the song text in their music books, students simultaneously hear the words and see them on paper. As students listen and sing, they begin to realize that the print contains meaning and that there are similarities within the print and the meaning.

In many instances, a teacher will incorporate the use of creative movement with singing to reinforce concepts of print. For example, we observed a teacher leading the folk song "Hawaiian Rainbows." As the children slowly read aloud each line of the song text in rhythm (by pointing to that text in their songbooks), the teacher asked for their ideas for simple arm movements to go with each line of the text. As the children carefully re-read the words to the song, they determined that four lines of text needed four different creative movements. Many children also noticed the rhyming words at the end of each phrase (by/sky and me/sea).

> Hawaiian rainbows, white clouds roll by;
> You show your colors against the sky.
> Hawaiian rainbows, it seems to me,
> Reach from the mountain down to the sea.

The teacher then taught the song's melody (line by line in echo fashion) and added the children's movement ideas. At the end of this lesson, the children were demonstrating their ability to appropriately master concepts of print within the active and expressive contexts of music and movement. Additionally, their total body involvement in the song's melody and movement served to heighten their understanding and enjoyment of the text. Illustrative activity, scenery design, and creative dramatic staging ideas could be a natural outgrowth of this activity.

A SENSE OF STORY AND SEQUENCE

A second important task for early readers to discern is the sense of story and sequence contained in narrative texts (e.g., Templeton, 1995). The earliest stories that children are likely to encounter are oral traditions and read-alouds. Understanding how stories work (in terms of their structure) "provides an inner model of the rhythms and patterns of written language" (Yaden, Smolkin, and Conlon, 1989, p. 208). As children begin to master the sense of story, more complex series of events are introduced. For example, classroom teachers use books to build students' understanding of story structures. A kindergarten teacher could start with *The Napping House* by Audrey Wood (1984) to create sense of sequence. The next book this teacher introduces might be *Drummer Hoff* by Barbara Emberly (1987) followed by *Possum Come a Knockin'* by Nancy Van Laan (1990). These books are highly musical both in their patterned rhyming text and rhythmical features.

Additionally, teachers can use some of the following examples of song/chant lyrics published as storybooks, including the following:

> *There Was an Old Lady Who Swallowed a Fly* illustrated by Pam Adams (Child's Play International, 1999)
> *There Was An Old Lady Who Swallowed a Fly* illustrated by Simms Taback (Viking, 1997)
> *Peanut Butter and Jelly* illustrated by Nadine Bernard Westcott (Dutton, 1987)
> *The Wheels on the Bus* adapted and illustrated by Paul Zelinsky (Dutton, 1990)
> *Little Rabbit Foo Foo* by Michael Rosen (Alladin, 1993)

Music contributes to students' understanding of stories and sequence. Songs that students learn each have a story to tell and teachers who integrate their curriculum enjoy building on this knowledge. In addition, several songs specifically address sequences. One teacher was observed leading the song "I Had an Old Coat," whose lyrics tells the story of a ragged old coat that gradually wears out and is made smaller and smaller into a jacket, a shirt, a vest, a tie, a patch, a button. Finally, when nothing is left of the old coat, the singer simply makes up a song!

As this teacher introduced the song's story sequence, she gave each child a piece of paper with a drawing of an old coat in the center of the page. The old coat illustration was surrounded by a border of labeled drawings of the other story components of the song text (jacket, button, etc.). The children in this class then sang along with the CD recording of "I Had an Old Coat" as they used bingo markers and checkers to move to the key word of each new verse. As they did so, they lightly tapped the song's steady beat onto the sheet of paper. For instance, when the song text read, "I stained that *vest* with cherry pie, So I cut and sewed 'til I had me a *tie*," the children would rhythmically (keeping the steady beat) move their markers from the vest to the tie. As an added bonus, the charming sequence theme of the song "I had an Old Coat" can be readily connected thematically to the Caldecott Award-winning book, *Joseph Had a Little Overcoat* by Simms Taback (1999), an Hawaiian version of the story found in *Auntie* by Stephany Indie (1998), as well as Patricia Polacco's (1998) popular book, *The Keeping Quilt.*

In another classroom observation, a well-known children's song, "I Know an Old Lady" was used to reinforce sequence. The lyrics began:

> I know an old lady who swallowed a fly;
> I don't know why she swallowed a fly. I guess she'll die.

The second verse continues with the lyric sequence "I know an old lady who swallowed a spider that wriggled and wriggled and tickled inside" which then adds the first verse in a cumulative style. As they sang, the children held up small paper cut-out characters attached to Popsicle sticks (fly, spider, bird, cat, dog, goat, cow, and horse) to show the song's evolving story sequence. On another day, the children sang the song again, this time demonstrating their understanding of sequence and their comprehension of the song lyrics by holding up word cards. Each card had an animal character name written on it and the children delighted in holding up their word cards at the appropriate time during the singing of the song. As they did so, they were required to find the next animal in the song, read their names, and organize their cards in a sequenced order—all within the enjoyable contexts of active music making.

In other classrooms, two children's books that use the same sequence story theme, *There was an Old Lady Who Swallowed a Fly* by Taback

(1997) and Adams (1999) were used first within dramatic/rhythmic group read-alouds and later as visual prompts during group singing and creative movements of the song, "I Know an Old Lady Who Swallowed a Fly." One teacher then added a CD recording of the King's Singers' humorous version of "I Know an Old Woman" within an extension listening lesson in which the children were asked to compare the recorded version to their song version. The children were delighted by the King's Singers' dazzling additions of the various animal character sounds!

PHONEMIC AWARENESS AND PHONICS

Phonemic awareness is believed to be a necessary precursor to reading (Adams, 1998) and an important component of a balanced early literacy program (Fisher, Lapp, and Flood, 1999; Yopp and Yopp, 1997). Accordingly, the Reading Language Arts Framework for California Schools states, "The most essential element of language arts instruction in kindergarten is the development of phonemic awareness; that is, teaching students the sound structure of language" (California Department of Education, 1999). Phonemic awareness occurs when students grasp the concept that letter sounds can be manipulated and recombined to create new words. Phonemic awareness differs from phonics in that the former focuses on sounds, not print. According to Ehri, Nunes, Willows, Schuster, Yaghoub-Zabeh, and Shanahan (2001, p. 253), the following tasks can be used for instruction in phonemic awareness:

- Phoneme *isolation*, which requires recognizing individual sounds in words; for example, "Tell me the first sound in taste." (/t/)
- Phoneme *identity*, which requires recognizing the common sound in different words; for example, "Tell me the sound that is the same in bike, boy, and bell." (/b/)
- Phoneme *categorization*, which requires recognizing the word with the odd sound in a sequence of three or four words; for example, "Which word does not belong in baby, bus, rug." (rug)
- Phoneme *blending*, which requires listening to a sequence of separately spoken sounds and combining them to form a recognizable word; for example, "What word is /s/ /t/ /o/ /p/?" (stop)
- Phoneme *segmentation*, which requires breaking a word into its sounds by tapping out or counting the sounds or by pronouncing and positioning a marker for each sound; for example, "How many phonemes in cat?" (3, /k/ /a/ /t/)

- Phoneme *deletion*, which requires recognizing what word remains when a specified phoneme is removed; for example, "What is smile without the /s/?" (mile)

In addition to phonemic awareness, students must learn how letters are used to represent speech sounds (Lapp and Flood, 1997). Phonics simply refers to the sounds that are used in English to convey meaning (phonemes) and the letters that represent those sounds (graphemes). The goal of phonics instruction is to move children to automaticity—or automatic word recognition—so that they can focus on meaning rather than decoding words. Phonics instruction often focuses on the sounds of each letter (e.g., /d/), the sounds of combinations of letters (e.g., /sh/ or /oo/), common spelling patterns (e.g., stop, hop, shop, slop), and long and short vowel patterns, to name a few.

Music is particularly useful in facilitating children's phonemic awareness. Teachers and parents also use illustrations, drawing, creative movement, and music for phonics instruction. For example, after his first graders finished chanting, "Engine, Engine," a teacher pointed out that there were many rhyming words in the chant. "Where are the rhyming words? What are they?"

> Engine, engine, number nine
> Rolling down Chicago line.
> See it sparkle, see it shine,
> Engine, engine number nine.

Once children had located these words, the teacher listed them within an outline of a giant train engine. After all of the rhyming words had been listed, the teacher and class created movements to each line of the chant. The teacher then lead the class in several games to heighten their awareness of the rhyming words. One was to ask the children to look at the chart as they moved and silently mouthed the words of each line. When the children came to the ending rhyming word of each line (nine, line, shine, and nine), they could say that word out loud together.

What better way than music to provide young children with a captivating entrance to the world of phonemes? Think of how we play with words within songs. Words are shortened, lengthened, repeated, sung high, low, loud, and soft. Lyrics are rhymed and altered in many ways—all connected to language play or language development.

BACKGROUND KNOWLEDGE AND VOCABULARY

Background knowledge and vocabulary are necessary for later reading and writing experiences. As Rosenblatt (1995) notes, readers bring a great deal of history to the text as they read. This transaction between the reader and the text is highly dependent on what the reader already knows. Classroom teachers often use thematic and interdisciplinary instruction to tie their lessons together and build on background knowledge. Classroom teachers also favor vocabulary lessons that are integrated into their thematic lessons.

As Gilles, Andre, Dye, and Pfannenstiel (1998) point out, students acquire new vocabulary and are introduced to fresh content each time they sing a song. For example, in the delightful story song, "The Crocodile," some students might not be familiar with the song text words, phrases, and concepts, "crocodile, tame as tame can be, down the Nile, bade them all goodbye." During another observation, a teacher listed these concepts, discussed their meaning, and encouraged the children to think of appropriate movements depicting their meanings. As the teacher returned to this same song on another day, she created a large story map chart asking the children to provide the WHO = a lady, WHERE = at the Nile River, WHEN = On a lovely summer day (components of the beginning section of the song story), the WHAT (happened) = the lady rides on the back of a friendly crocodile as she waved to people on the riverbank. The crocodile winked as he smiled . . . (components of the song text's middle section), as well as what happened at the end of the story. These kinds of early literacy/music teaching processes are a natural and frequently occurring instructional component prevalent in many classrooms that serve to heighten children's understanding of new vocabulary within meaningful, active, and expressive contexts.

BASIC SPELLING PATTERNS

Spelling remains a challenge for many students. It is important for early readers to understand that the English language has a number of word families and that these word families are based on specific spelling patterns. One of the ways that classroom teachers teach basic spelling patterns is through the use of word sort activities (e.g., Abouzeid, Invernizzi, Bear, and Ganske, 2000). Word sort activities range from sorting words by their first letter, to sorting words by topics, to sorting words by ending spelling patterns.

With second grade music students, a teacher used the song "In the Barnyard" as part of his music program. He had written all the words from the song that ended with -alk, -ound, or -oud on sentence strips. He asked his students to sort the cards by spelling pattern: all of the words with -ound, for example, were to be placed in the same column. As a distracter because he knew his students well, he added a few words that did not fit into one of the three spelling patterns and observed if students would leave those cards out.

Other examples of the use of basic spelling patterns in music are easy to find. For instance, in another classroom, a teacher used the song "Free at Last" to focus on the word sort for the spelling patterns -alk and -air. In addition to asking students to sort the words from the song, she invited them to identify additional words with the spelling pattern and write them on cards. When small groups of students had done so, they passed their cards to another group for this new group to sort.

Another useful and creative song for word sort activity, "I Can't Spell Hippopotamus," includes a variety of two-letter word families or phonemes. The lyrics to this song include many rhyming words, such as: hat/fat/cat/mat, hog/dog/log, etc. Children are delighted to spell out loud and creatively move to their new rhyming word discoveries. One teacher we observed used this song at a listening station and invited her students to use the onset and rhyme cards to create lists of words from the song.

CONCLUSION

Now is the time to make known the natural links between arts activities and important instructional goals in literacy. The instructional strategies used during language arts time, especially during emergent literacy, can be enhanced with the arts. We are especially interested in the use of music for literacy development. To help communicate this important information with other teachers, parents, and administrators, teachers might find it helpful to use the information listed in table 3.1 by adding to it their own examples (song and chant material, texts, storybooks, poetry, etc.) of what they already do in their classrooms using each of the literacy concepts within musical contexts. After completing the table, teachers could begin a dialogue with others as they share its content with teaching colleagues and administrators.

Table 3.1.   Early Literacy Components and Music Teacher Resources
(*Idea for usage: Copy this table and insert your own curriculum materials to share with classroom teachers, parents, other music teachers, administrators, and curriculum coordinators)

Early Literacy Component	Recommendations from The Music Connection © 1995, 2000 (Silver Burdett Ginn)	Additional Music Sources Used in Your Classroom (*fill in your own ideas here)
Concepts of print	Hawaiian Rainbows Ev'rybody Ought to Know This Old Man Time to Sing ABC Rock I Got a Letter This Morning	
A sense of story and sequence	I Had an Old Coat I Know an Old Lady Oliver Twist (chant) Brush Your Teeth Hush Little Baby Farmer in the Dell Jack and Jill (chant)	
Phonemic awareness and phonics	Engine, Engine (chant) Ackabacka, Soda Cracker (chant) Bingo Apples and Bananas Button, You Must Wander	
Background knowledge and vocabulary	The Crocodile I Had an Old Coat Abiyoyo The Sun Hawaiian Rainbows	
Basic spelling patterns	In the Barnyard Free at Last I Can't Spell Hippopotamus	
Early writing activities	Miss White Had a Fright (chant) In las Pulgas de San Jose Abiyoyo	

Questions for further discussion, study, and project development:

- What are the commonalties and differences between read-alouds, shared reading, guided reading, and independent reading?
- How can the arts be used within read-alouds, shared reading, guided reading, independent reading, and writing instruction?

- What are some ways that the arts can be utilized to help teach each of the following: concepts of print, sense of story and sequence, phonemic awareness and phonics, background knowledge and vocabulary, and spelling?
- Using the ideas in this chapter, what creative arts and literacy activities might you select to implement with the book *Sadako* (about the girl who made peace cranes in Japan after the bombing of Hiroshima) or another book frequently used in your classroom?

ADDITIONAL SOURCES

Barnett, P., Fisher, D., Hamblin, M., Johnson, S., McDonald, N., and Strickland, J. (2000). *Emergent literacy through music: Grade 2 folders: Phonemic awareness review, Speaking and writing: telling, retelling, and dramatizing, Purposeful listening, Awareness of words, syllables, and sentences, Comprehension and critical thinking, Manipulating phonemes and spelling*. New Jersey: Pearson Education—Scott Foresman, Silver Burdett Ginn Music.

Ericson, L., and Juliebo, M. F. (1998). *The phonological awareness handbook for kindergarten and primary teachers*. Newark, Del.: International Reading Association.

Foye, M. M., and Lacroix, S. E. (1998). "Making connections through integrated curriculum." *National Association of Laboratory Schools Journal*, 22(3), 1–4.

Herchold, T., and Johnson, S. (2000). *Emergent literacy through music: Grade K folders: Concepts of print, Sensitivity to rhyme, Purposeful listening, Initial consonant sounds, Manipulating phonemes, Awareness of words and syllables*. New Jersey: Pearson Education—Scott Foresman, Silver Burdett Ginn Music.

Herchold, T., and Johnson, S. (2000). *Emergent literacy through music: Grade 1 folders: Concepts of print, Sensitivity to rhyme, Purposeful listening, Initial consonant sounds, Manipulating phonemes, Awareness of words and syllables*. New Jersey: Pearson Education—Scott Foresman, Silver Burdett Ginn Music.

Jalongo, M. R., and Ribblett, D. M. (1997). "Using picture books to support emergent literacy." *Childhood Education, 74*, 15–22.

Levene, D. (1993). *Music through children's literature: Theme and variations*. Englewood, Colo.: Teacher Ideas Press.

McCracken, R., and McCracken, M. (1998). *Stories, song, and poetry to teach reading and writing.* Winnipeg, Manitoba: Peguis.

Tarlow, E. (1998). *Teaching story elements with favorite books: Creative and engaging activities to explore character, plot, setting, and theme: Grades 1–3.* New York: Scholastic.

CHAPTER 4

How Can Poetry Be Made Exciting for My Students?

Poetry often enters through the window of irrelevance.

—M. C. Richards

Tell me, I forget
Show me, I remember
Involve me, I understand

—Chinese Proverb

Herein lies the historical problem with teaching poetry. All too often students are required to memorize poetry and recite it to the teacher. Then they forget the poems the next day. Because the students were not involved with the poem text—through movement, expressive speech, performance, or context of the poem—they didn't understand it. They haven't felt the poetry nor developed a way to understand what the poet was trying to convey. Teachers who teach children poetry through creative and evocative active experiences allow children to enter into the meaningful and artistically expressive nature of the poetry itself. Total physical involvement in artistic "recreations" of that poem (through the use of creative movement, drama, music, and visual art) allow children to become intimately involved in the poetry. The poet's language becomes:

> part of the child's real world in which speaking, singing, poetry and music, playing and dancing are not yet separated . . . They are essentially one and indivisible, all governed by the play instinct . . . for the child language is not . . . abstract . . . but is of the same stuff as his play, his gestures, and his images. (Landis and Carder, 1972, p. 99)

This chapter focuses on the use of poetry in the classroom. First, readers are provided with a sample lesson in which poetry is the focus of the integrated arts lesson. Although haiku is used in this particular lesson, other types of poetry can be taught using this format. Following the haiku lesson is a primary grade example of the use of poetry integrated into a classroom theme—this time focused on the theme of transportation. After that, we turn to the upper grades for a look inside a classroom in which poetry and science have been integrated using the award-winning book of poetry titled *Joyful Noise*.

TEACHING THE GENRE OF POETRY: FOCUSING ON HAIKU

One form of poetry is the Japanese art of haiku writing (Navasky, 1993). Haiku poems consist of three unrhymed lines of text, with a total of seventeen syllables. Haiku, if written masterfully, moves. The form offers spaces for our own thoughts and designs. One senses its setting, a season, a moment in which delicate outlines of action and reflection are offered to the reader. Classic haiku reflects the simplicity and beauty of line found in the painting and music of the great Japanese masters. Students often have a difficult time understanding these elements and thus the significance of haiku when it is not taught as a creative, artistic experience (Rielly, 1988).

Setting the Scene with Movement

Slow-tempo Koto (Japanese zither) and Shakuhachi (flute) music is playing softly in the background. We begin by having the students silently mirror the ultra-slow, very connected movements of the teacher. "Now silently find a partner, alternating who leads the movement. The follower must mirror the actions exactly, even if the leader chooses to take the movement to the floor level, or move the ideas across the room." Insist that the movement be connected and slow, as if underwater. The teacher may give quiet cues (i.e., "Move in a low space," "Move with your partner across the floor space," or "Now change to the other leader," cueing the students with a wind chime or other quiet sound).

Keep the music playing. Show pictures of classic Japanese watercolors, watercolors with poetry characters, flower arrangements, Zen gardens, etc. (e.g., The Metropolitan Museum of Art, 1985). Talk about simplicity and beauty of designs. Explain how many Japanese poets were also artists and musicians.

The Poetry

Keep the music on. Quietly tell the students that you have decided to create "scenes" for haiku. Next the teacher models a selected haiku, for instance,

> A flash of lightning . . .
> the sound of dew
> dripping down the bamboo

The teacher models the haiku in three distinct ways:

1. *Speaking only* Use highly expressive/dramatic speech that varies the tempo (speed) and dynamics (softs and louds) according to the feeling and meaning of the words.
2. *Dramatic speech with movement*   Repeat the haiku, but this time add simple movements to the mood of the expressive speech. For instance, "flash!" might be a jagged double-arm movement that "freezes" in space. The "dew" could be a spiraling movement descending to the floor as if drops were actually winding their way down bamboo.
3. *Movement only*   Think the words, even mouth them if necessary, while performing the haiku movements without sound. Have the students try the movement sequence with you once. Discuss how the poetry comes alive with movement.

Assign groups of four students, give each student a copy of several haiku poems, and then give the following directions (see table 4.1 for samples):

"Read several haiku poems aloud with your group before you decide on one. Each group will select their own haiku to perform. Create a haiku "scene" with expressive speech, movement and speech, and then movement alone [List instructions on the board]. When you have practiced your three ways of performing your haiku and feel you are ready, come to me and I'll give you paper and art supplies to draw a scene or backdrop for your haiku. We will be performing our haiku for each other in about twenty-five minutes."

Table 4.1. Sample Haiku Poems (From the Great Japanese Master Poets)

One fallen flower
returning to the branch?
. . . Oh no!
A white butterfly
    —Moritak

Under cherry-trees . . .
soup, the salad, fish and all . . .
seasoned with petals
    —Basho

Pretty butterflies . . .
Be careful of pine-needle points
in this gusty wind!
    —Shusen

Darting dragon-fly . . .
Pull off its shiny wings and look . . .
Bright red pepper-pod
    —Kikaku

Friend, that open mouth
Reveals your whole interior . . .
Silly hollow frog!
    —Anon.

I am going out . . .
Be good and play together
My cricket children
    —Issa

Over the mountain
Bright the full white
moon now smiles on the
flower-thief
    —Issa

Lady butterfly
perfumes her wings
by floating over the orchard
    —Basho

May rains!
Now frogs are swimming
at my door
    —Sanpu

Oh do not swat them . . .
unhappy flies
forever wringing their thin hands
    —Issa

A blind child
guided by his mother,
admires the cherry blossoms
    —Kikaku

Ha! the butterfly!
—it is following the person
who stole the flowers!
    —Anon.

Finally, gather the actors/movers/artists together. Let them know that each group will unroll their "scenery" and perform their poetry in the three ways (speaking only, dramatic speaking with movement, and movement only). End the performance with all the haiku groups performing their movement-only sequence all at the same time. Use recorded music throughout and fade at the very end.

Writing Haiku

Now that the students have an understanding of haikus, lead a class discussion about the characteristics of haiku. Students should note that the poems relate to seasons and have movement. Explain the traditional seventeen-syllable structure of haiku. The first line consists of five syllables and sets the scene or environment for the poem. The second line has seven syllables and the third line has five syllables. These two lines typically feature an action or movement that is unending and leaves the reader wondering. Invite groups to write and illustrate their own haiku. These poems should be performed using the same three-step process. Students might also wish to create some of the following: a photo-essay related to the poem, a theater presentation of the haiku model with narration between the scenes (poems), original scenery and costumes for each of the poems, and/or student-created music compositions coordinated with the group movements. Follow-up with students by inviting them to write individual journal reflections about their experiences with haiku.

POETRY WITHIN A THEMATIC UNIT: TRANSPORTATION—PRIMARY GRADES

Transportation is a popular theme in the primary grades. Teachers across the country focus on travel in the air, on land, or at sea during their kindergarten and first grade social studies lessons. Students in grades two and three rarely receive deeper instruction about transportation. However, we know that these seven- to nine-year-olds remain very interested in how people move from place to place. Children love to write, draw, and create dramatic interpretations of their transportation experiences. For example, Justin visited his grandmother and desperately wanted to tell the class about the various forms of transportation he used to get there, including a commuter train. He wrote in his journal "I sat at the window and I could see everything go by. The train went through big tunnels, drove over mountains, and went very fast right by the ocean. When we were next to the freeway, we were going faster than the trucks. We stopped at seven towns before I got to my grandmother's house. I learned the name of all the towns."

Justin's third grade teacher realized that her students rarely had the opportunity to express their excitement and wonderings about travel. Justin's teacher shared Justin's journal with her colleagues during lunch. They all agreed that Justin's writing was unusually rich and hypothesized, and that this was probably because of his interest in the topic. One of the teachers at this lunch suggested that Justin's teacher visit the school library and borrow the book *Train Song* (Siebert, 1990) to give to him that afternoon. Seeing his excitement after reading a book related to his travel experiences, Justin's teacher, Ms. Noriega, decided to create an integrated thematic unit of study about trains. She used the genre of poetry so that she could meet a literacy standard along the way.

The Lesson Begins

Ms. Noriega began her discussion about trains by asking her students the following questions as she listed their responses on a chart:

- Where can we see trains? What kinds of trains pass through our town?
- Where are those trains going? What are they carrying?
- What are some things we see, hear, and feel as we watch trains go by?
- What are some things we see, hear, and feel when we go on a train ride?

The children became very engaged in sharing what they already knew about trains. As they shared their responses, the teacher would prompt more discussion by asking:

- What kinds of things might be inside the train's cargo bins?
- When does the engineer sound the train horn? Why?
- How is the train powered?
- What makes its wheels turn?
- Do you start a train like you start a car, with a key?

These kinds of probes resulted in even more student participation and descriptive phrases to add to the class "All About Trains" chart.

After this discussion, the teacher asked the students to illustrate various descriptive phrases listed on the chart. For instance, Pilar chose to illustrate the phrases "giant wheels on rails of steel" and "cargo bins full of grain." The teacher encouraged class members to each illustrate different chart ideas so that their illustrations could reflect the content of the "All About Trains" class chart. The students' individual phrases and illustrations were compiled into a class book, which was bound and added to the class library.

Introducing Poetry into the Unit

Following this, Ms. Noriega read aloud *Train Song* by Diane Siebert (1990). This book contains beautiful illustrations within highly evocative, poetic text about the sights, sounds, and rhythmic energy of trains and train travel. The children then read aloud the book's text as a readers' theater, first all together and then in small groups with individuals assigned to certain pages. The children were encouraged to find ways to make the poetry come alive as the teacher modeled the following text with dramatic expression and creative movement:

> steel wheels rolling
> on steel trails
> rumbling
> grumbling
> on steel rails

She read aloud other rhythmical sections of the text and asked the students to echo back her voice model of these sections in rhythm. She then asked the children for ideas for simple movements to accompany that text. The students particularly enjoyed choral speaking and creatively moving to the following section of the text:

> great trains
> freight trains
> talk about your late trains
> the 509
> right on time
> straight through to L.A.
> whistle blows

there she goes
slicing through the day

Ms. Noriega pointed out that train sounds can also be very entertaining. She asked her students to listen to the delightful King's Singers' recording of the song "I'm a Train" (see the resource list in table 4.2). The students were asked how they thought the singers created realistic sounds and motions of a train with their voices. Several of the students were able to recreate some of the amusing vocables used to capture the sound of the train's wheels, whistle, and changing speed. This recording was so popular with the students that they requested to hear it time and time again.

Integrating Arts into the Lesson

By now, the students had thought about, discussed, read aloud, moved to, visualized, and illustrated concepts about trains. The teacher then led the children in a guided musical listening experience using the orchestral composition, "Pacific 231," by the composer Honneger (see the resource list in table 4.2). This twentieth century piece is a musical representation of the sounds and rhythms of a modern locomotive's journey over the rails. To guide the students through the action or sections of this six-minute recording, the teacher created six "guidepost signs" for the children to read aloud before listening to the piece:

1. The engine is at a standstill, gathering steam.
2. The big wheels begin to slowly turn as the locomotive gets under way.
3. The locomotive begins to move more quickly, gathering speed as it goes.
4. The sleek silver train rushes through the dark night.
5. The great engine slows down.
6. The great steel wheels finally grind to a stop.

As the recording of "Pacific 231" played, the teacher held up the "guidepost" of the appropriate section of the piece. The students were asked to silently read the sign as the music was playing. They then closed their eyes to listen, visualize, and write down their ideas about how the train might look and sound during this section of the music. Between guidepost four and five is a longer listening section during which the students were asked to illustrate their visualization of the train as it "rushed

Table 4.2. Resource List for Transportation Unit

Books

Aylesworth, J. (1991). *Country crossing*. New York: Athenean Books.
Sights and sounds of a powerful freight train as it passes a country railroad crossing on
  a summer night. The whole scene is witnessed lovingly by an old man and a little boy
  who wait patiently in their car at the railroad crossing. Rich in sound scapes and
  vocabulary. Excellent for a study of dynamics, louds and softs in music and
  movement, visual art, and speech/drama.

Cooney, B. (1982). *Miss Rumphius*. New York: Viking.
A former town librarian tells her story of the adventurous travel excitement of her youth.
  Text and charming illustrations can be used for discussion and writing extensions
  about places the students would like to go, and people they know who have traveled
  to many interesting places.

Fraser, M. A. (1993). *Ten mile day and the building of the transcontinental railroad*. New
  York: Henry Holt.
A well-researched account for 3–6th grade readers of the building of the
  Transcontinental Railroad's last 10 miles in the Spring of 1869. Excellent information
  on the geography, biography, events, and historical viewpoints including Chinese
  Laborers, Native Americans, business management, and journalistic accounts of the
  exciting meeting of the rails.

Hartry, N. (1997). *Hold on, McGinty!* New York: Doubleday.
The cross-Canada adventure of an old fisherman who must relocate (with his boat!)
  from his beloved home on the Newfoundland Atlantic coast westward to his
  daughter's home on Vancouver Island. To get there, McGinty rides inside his boat on a
  freight train.

Heap, C. (1998). *Big book of trains*. New York: DK Publishing.
The book has a gigantic format—more than 50 trains. Steam engines, diesel to modern
  electric trains, bullet trains around the world. Focus is on both human drivers and
  operators as well as computer technologies. Shows the evolution of trains and rail
  transport.

Morris, A. (1990). *On the go*. New York: Lothrop, Lee, and Shepard.
Beautiful photographs feature many kinds of transportation around the world.

Poetry

Livingston, M. C. (Ed.). (1993). *Roll along: Poems on wheels*. New York: Margaret
  McElderry.
Fifty poems in this anthology about transportation—bikes, skateboards, cars, buses,
  trucks, jeeps, subways, wagons, motorcycles, etc., as well as travel modes kids can
  only dream about! Many unique sounds, words, and rhythms as well as created
  words to imitate or capture the sights and sounds of the transport. Great resource!

Peet, B. (1971). *The caboose who got loose*. New York: Houghton Mifflin.
Melodic prose. The caboose of a train hates always being last! An accident happens
  and she gets perched between two evergreen trees.

Prelutsky, J. (1983). *The Random House book of poetry for children*. New York: Random
  House.
Contains many poems about transportation themes. Look for "Sing a Song of Subways"
  by Eve Merriam and "Things to Do If You Are a Subway" by Bobbi Katz.

Siebert, D. (1981). *Train song*. New York: HarperCollins.
Excellent poetic text and beautiful illustrations rich in sound descriptions and sensory stimuli. Excellent for reading and read alouds. Great potential for movement, dramatization, and prompts for visual art and creative writing.

Suen, A. (1998). *Window music*. New York: Viking.
"Window Music" is railroad slang for the passing scenery. The book is full of simple rhyme and beautiful, rich earth-toned illustrations. The train makes "music" through the rhyme and rhythm of the text. Conveys a girl's train ride home from her grandparents' house. Travels through all types of terrain and then to the final destination of a city train depot.

Music

- The following song and poetry material is from *The Music Connection*, K–8 National Music Series by Scott Foresman/Silver Burdett and Ginn Music (©1995, 2000) Parsippany, New Jersey, and from *Making Music* (© 2002) by the same publisher.
- Songs may be used at any appropriate grade level determined by text difficulty and musical content. CD's may be a great help. Poetry selections are printed in the Teacher and Student texts, but are not recorded on CD's. Also, song texts may be used as poetry.

Song Title	*SBG* The Music Connection Grade, TE pg, CD #	*SBG* Making Music Grade, TE pg, CD #
Chicka Hanka		2, pg. 207, CD 7–7
Engine, Engine (chant)	K, pg. 305	
Freight Train		1, pg. 46, CD 1–51
Get on Board	2, pg. 58, CD 2–25	K, pg. 89, CD 3–30
Going Places (poem)	K, pg. 89	
How Long the Train Been Gone?	2, pg. 263, CD 8–11	
I've Been Working on the Railroad		3, pg. 238, CD 7–14
Little Red Caboose	K, pg. 200, CD 5–5	K, pg. 229, CD 7–30
Long Trip (poem)	5, pg. 70	
Long Way Home, A	1, pg. 149, CD 4–4	
Morningtown ride	K, pg. 228, CD 5–38	
Nine Hundred Miles	5, pg. 202, CD 9–1	
Paige's Train	K, pg. 312, CD 7–31	
Railroad Cars Are Coming (poem)	4, pg. 141	
The Rock Island Line	4, pg. 140, CD 6–3	4, pg. 52, CD 2–24
Same Train	2, pg. 122, CD 4–14	2, pg. 162, CD 5–33
She'll Be Comin' Round the Mountain		2, pg. 344, CD 11–32
Travel Plans (poem)	K, pg. 163	
Wabash Cannon Ball	5, pg. 208, CD 9–9	2, pg. 132, CD 6–1
When the Train Comes Along	1, pg. 148, CD 4–3	1, pg. 286, CD 8–2

Table 4.2. (continued)   Resource List for Transportation Unit

Musical Listening Examples for Transportation Themes:
All examples are found within *The Music Connection* (K–8 National Text Series) by
   Scott Foresman / Silver Burdett Ginn © 1995, 2000

Song Title	*SBG* The Music Connection Grade, TE pg, CD #
"Blue Town, New York Montage" from *Moscow on the Hudson* by McHugh	4, pg. 41, CD 2–14
"I'm a Train" by the King's Singers	4, pg. 141, CD 6–4
"Little Red Caboose" by Sweet Honey in the Rock	K, pg. 200, CD 5–6
"The Little Train of the Caipira" from Bachianas Brasileiras No. 2 by Villa-Lobos	2, pg. 123, CD 4–15
"Pacific 231" (modern train) by Honegger	4, pg. 142, CD 6–5"
"There's a Morning Train A-Comin'" by Eddleman	1, pg. 66, CD 2–11

Videos

Lots & Lots of Trains Vol. 1 (1999). ASIN: 1581681259
This video contains some of the most exciting trains you'll ever see! In this volume,
   you'll see lots of trains winding through mountains, climbing steep grades, gliding
   over tracks, hauling, pulling, loading and much more!

Kids Love Trains (1994). ASIN: 6303257577
This train video shows many types of trains. My children love the songs and music in
   this video. You'll enjoy watching this one with your child.

through the night." Even though this fourth guidepost section is the
longest of the entire piece, the students were focused throughout the musical listening lesson because of the instruction that accompanied it.

After hearing the entire piece, the children shared what they imagined, wrote, or illustrated during each "guidepost" section. Maria
wrote, "Pacific 231 was a powerful train. It took a lot of time for it to
get going, but then I could hear how fast it could go. When it slowed
down, I pretended I was at the train station waiting for my uncle to get
off the train. Then I ran to meet him!" Kyle wrote, "Pacific 231 had to
go up hills, through lots of tunnels and up and down mountains. Its
horn blasted a lot through the night. People in towns were really mad
when the train woke them up. When it finally came to a stop, all the en-
gineers needed to take a nap before their next trip."

Ms. Noriega knew that many students in her class had learned the famous song "I've Been Working on the Railroad" in their music classes.
With guidance from the music teacher, she knew that the children had

already created movements and classroom instrument accompaniments for this song. The students incorporated some of the vocables from the King's Singers' recording (e.g., "chuck-a, chuck-a" and "ssshhh") into their singing of "I've Been Working on the Railroad." Ms. Noriega quickly realized she had unleashed a significant amount of creativity!

At this point, student interest in trains had grown considerably. Ania, an avid Harry Potter reader, raised her hand during class one day and excitedly shared that even Harry rides a train (the Hogwarts Express) to wizard school! Guiding the conversation back to the history of trains and railroads, Ms. Noriega introduced a wonderful book about the history of trains and railroads, *Steam, Smoke and Steel: Back in Time with Trains* by Patrick O'Brien (2000). The text is presented through the voice of a young boy who decides to become a railroad engineer, just as his past seven generations of family had done. The boy tells the story, aided by accurate historical photographs and interesting railroad lore, of each of his relatives and the trains they loved and rode. The students were fascinated with the photos of historic trains. Jamika commented, "I've seen a steam engine like that at the railroad museum! That other one looks like the train at Disneyland."

Not only were the students interested in modern trains and train travel, they began asking questions about all kinds of trains, past and present. Once the children were familiar with the look of old trains, the teacher drew their attention to a map of the United States. As she began to introduce the traditional American folksong "The Wabash Cannon Ball," she pointed out that there are a lot of tall tales about famous trains, and that those tall tales have been added to as time goes on. The tale of the Wabash Cannon Ball has evolved over the years to include ideas about where this fantasy train might go, mysterious names of the IJA&SM Railroad on which it ran (Ireland, Jerusalem, Australia, and Southern Michigan Railroad!) and that it was once owned by the younger brother of Paul Bunyan, Cal Bunyan. The Wabash Cannon Ball was once said to have 700 cars and a ticket collector who had to ride a motorcycle over the top of the train to collect all the passenger tickets. The mysterious train was known to travel so fast that it was seen arriving at its destination an hour before it even left the station! (Silver, Burdett, & Ginn, 1995).

The students began to spontaneously add to the "Wabash Cannon Ball" tall tale with ideas of their own. Kim giggled, "The Wabash Cannon Ball was so long that the engine would be in California when its caboose was in Texas!" Ramona added "The Wabash Cannon Ball gave off so much steam, it caused a flood in Kansas." The teacher asked the children to write down their tall-tale ideas to create a "tall tale" narration to accompany a performance of the song they were about to learn.

As children pointed to their music texts, they then read aloud the verses and refrain of the "Wabash Cannon Ball" song. The students pointed to the words as they read aloud. After reading aloud rhythmically, the children listened to the CD recording of the song as they continued to point to the song text and they mouthed the words. Quickly, the children began to sing along on the refrain:

> Just listen to the jingle, the rumble, and the roar
> Of the mighty locomotive as she streams along the shore,
> Hear the thunder of the engine, hear the lonesome whistle call,
> It's the Western combination called the *Wabash Cannon Ball*.

The teacher then asked the students to find all the names of cities and other places mentioned in the song. Eagerly, the children offered, "Pacific, Atlantic, Southland, Labrador, Chicago, Saint Louis, Rock Island and Santa Fe," and found their locations on the map in order to trace the route of this mysterious, mythical train. Jason asked, "Wow! How could one train go all those places?" The class laughed and reminded him that it was a tall-tale train!

The Transportation Performance

The class became excited about sharing their creative ideas about trains with other classes. Given that first graders at her school all studied transportation, Ms. Noriega asked her colleagues if they would like to attend a special transportation performance staged by her third grade class. In addition to the poem "Trains and Trucks and Planes" (see table 4.3), the class decided to share the following activities with the younger students:

- A sing-along performance of "I've Been Working on the Railroad"
- A read-aloud of the class book of poems and illustrations
- A readers' theater performance of *Train Song*
- A lip-sync of "I'm a Train"
- Narration of interesting facts from history books and Internet searches
- Singing and tall tales of "The Wabash Cannon Ball"
- An improvised creative movement and instrument sound activity for the younger students in which they become trains and travel around the room
- A sentence about trains dictated by the first grader to a third grade buddy, illustrated and bound into a first grade class library book

Table 4.3. "Trains and Trucks and Planes" by Nan McDonald

Over rails and roads and sky
There's adventure for a watchful eye
When I'm alone and bored or blue
I plan a trip for me and you . . .

A trip by rail would be just fine
Big engine pulling train cars in line
Our window seats provide a view
Of endless chances to see something new

Big rig gleaming over wheels so high
Horn blasting "hello" to cars passing by
A truck trip would be so great
But big deliveries just can't be late!

We could soar above cities, hills, and all below
In our plane traveling isn't as slow
Mountains, deserts, islands, and sea
The whole world waits for you and me.

POETRY WITHIN A THEMATIC UNIT: INSECTS—UPPER GRADES

It should be clear by now that we value playfulness and experimentation with poetry. We believe that through total-body movement, playfulness, and experimentation, children can more deeply experience and remember poems. As you have seen, many curriculum areas can become integrated in this process, including the arts, literature, language arts, and science (see chapter 2). Curricular integration of this sort is not merely a clever usage of a popular educational buzzword, but rather a purposeful "suite" of learning activities whose doors all open to a "main room," the poem itself.

Now we turn to integrated curriculum for older students. The purpose of this lesson is to offer suggestions for artistic activities and curricular connections that might deepen your students' interest and enjoyment of insects through the collection of poems found in *Joyful Noise: Poems for Two Voices* by Paul Fleischman (1988). Lesson ideas are to be thought of as suggestions to be incorporated over an extended period of time.

Joyful Noise, by nature, is a performance piece, rich in both musical and dramatic expression. It was meant to be read out loud, in two voices reading separate columns of the page. Some lines are performed in unison, some in counterpoint. The poems demand the direct, spoken participation of all readers. Its meanings are rooted in **how** the words sound out loud, the resulting rich colorations of the language's sound, dynamics (louds and softs), and tempi (speed). *Joyful Noise*'s artistic sound components create a musical, choral activity.

Readers quite naturally become the actors, the insect characters. Many poems in *Joyful Noise* have a distinct sense of accent, articulation, and accelerando/ritardando (a gradual speeding up and slowing down of movement, if you will). Each poem's contents create a wide variety of expressive moods. Many poems seem to beg for accompanying interpretive movement and gesture. Additionally, *Joyful Noise* has powerfully beautiful, humorous, and sometimes poignant illustrations that could be used in soliciting your students' ideas about the poetry.

Science offers interesting avenues of understanding why the poems' insects speak and act as they do. Understanding the insects' "place" in our environment could be paramount to understanding the poem itself. Within *Joyful Noise* is a goldmine of potential discussion topics that lead children toward creative writing about the book's characters and action. The curiosity generated by direct participation in a performance "recreation" of the poem could be a catalyst for your students to read more literature with insect themes.

Production Notes

Setting the Scene: (Grades 4–8)

Although *Joyful Noise* was written for children, its sophisticated metaphor and illustrative character action might require some thoughtful precursor activity designed to increase your students' interest and involvement in the meaning of the poetry. The following is a series of opening activities (curriculum connections) utilizing language arts, reading, literature, science, creative writing, visual art, music, theater and dance.)

Science/Language Arts Connections

Play a nature-sound recording (see the sources in table 4.4) as you begin a dialogue with students about insects. Questions you might ask include: Insects have always interested me. How about you? How do you feel about insects? What words describe how you feel when you think of insects? Ask the students what words or phrases come to mind when they think about bugs (e.g., creepy, "kill them," mysterious, swarming, nighttime). List all suggestions on the board. Ask the students what they already know about insects. The students can individually share out loud (or with partners) by making lists of the kinds of insects they are familiar with, including where they live, what they do, what they look like, and how they feel about them. Collect as many descriptors as you can and save them. Then ask the students what they

Table 4.4.   Music and Dance Resources for the Insect Unit

The following musical selections can be found in classical sections of local record stores. Look for them by finding the composer's last name.

"Dance of the Mosquito" by Anatol Liadov
"Le Jardin du Ferrique" (the Fairy Garden) by Maurice Ravel
"Flight of the Bumble Bee" by Rimsky-Korsakov
"Night of the Electric Insects" by George Crum
"Nights in the Garden of Spain" by Daphalla

Have the children listen carefully for "soundscapes" that remind them in some way of their learning about insect life and behavior. Compare and contrast the pieces. Have the children draw listening maps, illustrations, or write key words and phrases that come to mind as they listen. Tell the children that ". . .we may be using this music during our presentation of *Joyful Noise*. When should we use this music? How? What should be going on during the music? What does the music seem to depict about the life of insects?"

Music for Sound Effects or Background
Nature recordings (sounds) with no added music. Suggestion: Look for recordings of night sounds, crickets, forest at night, etc. Good source: Nature Company tapes and CDs.

Music for a Created Cricket Dance
Fresh Air III by Mannheim Steamroller, American Gramophone Records or CDs, Omaha, Nebraska, 1979. Copyright by Dots and Links, Inc.
"The Cricket" is from the section of the recording entitled "The Woods is Alive!" The music is 2 minutes and 25 seconds in length and features a live cricket chirping throughout. Apparently the cricket was in the recording studio during production. Mannheim Steamroller credits this performer as "Claudette Criquet (no longer with us) . . . Everyone was most impressed with her impeccable rhythm and incredible control of dynamics."

still want to learn about insects; allow them to share out loud, thus creating the first two parts of the KWL (Ogle, 1986).

Students can then go on an insect "discovery mission" (alone or in teams). They will search around the school buildings and grounds until they find an insect. In their newly created bug journal, students can draw a map of the twenty-five-foot radius of where an insect was found and answer the bug journal questions suggested in table 4.5.

Visual Arts Connection

Each student could also draw the found insect, identify it by using a science book source, and draw (illustrate) its immediate environment in their journals. Students should observe the insect for fifteen minutes in that environment, ideally on more than one occasion. Journal discoveries can be shared with the entire class, perhaps displayed on a theme bulletin board.

Table 4.5.   Bug Journal Questions

1. As you watch the insects, ask yourself these questions:

   - What are they doing?
   - Do they work in groups or independently?
   - Is this location their home or are they just passing through?
   - What is their home like?
   - What are they eating?
   - What eats them?
   - How do they defend themselves?
   - Do they bite, flee, freeze, or burrow?
   - How does their behavior change during your visit?

2. Draw sketches of the insects you find noting any interesting features.
3. Identify the plants that attract insects.

   - What bugs prefer what plants?
   - How do they use those plants?
   - Do they eat them?
   - What part do they eat?
   - Does the plant provide a home for the insect?

Source: Booth, J. (1994). *Big bugs: Getting to know little creatures up close.* San Diego: Harcourt Brace. (Page 4)

Some teachers will want to share information about insect themes found in artwork of multiple cultures (see the art sources in table 4.6). The teacher might ask, "How is this Japanese ink drawing of a cricket different than the Australian Aborigine painting?" Students can study how Aborigines depicted insects as spiritual guides in their dream-world paintings, or how insects were often depicted in traditional Chinese and Japanese art and poetry. As you show artwork, ask the students, "What are the insects doing in the artwork? How does this depiction match up with what we know about these insects? Do you think the artist likes insects? Why? Why not? Are the insects depicted within their natural setting? Why? Why not? How would you draw your favorite insect within a creative environment, a comical environment, or a natural environment? What colors would you use? What would your insect be doing?" "Let's draw our insects creatively, or in natural settings." Display the student work and save it.

Music and Dance Connections

Teachers might also wish that insects were an inspiration for expression in other arts. Music with insects themes could be played as children create listening maps and later discuss how the music depicts characteristics of those insects' movement and habitat (see the music sources in table 4.4).

Table 4.6. Curricular Connections Sources of Information: Insect Themes

Reference	Summary
Booth, J. (1994). *Big bugs: Getting to know little creatures up close*. San Diego: Harcourt Brace.	SCIENCE. This is a great source of scientific information on bugs, habitats, projects involving finding and observing bugs, ecology-sensitive projects, experiments and ideas for environmental protection and preservation, the role of bugs in the environment, and even bug art and cooking ideas!!! Stories about real children who are involved in nature projects, and solving environmental problems in their own neighborhoods. Oversized with beautiful lithographs, color illustrations, and technical renditions of bugs. Great for all grades, readable, usable by kids in grades 3-7.
Cassedy, S., & Suetake, K. (1992). *Red dragonfly on my shoulder*. New York: HarperCollins.	ART and POETRY. Many haiku about insects imaginatively surrounded by original collages that may suggest art projects for students.
Claudhill, R. (1964). *A pocketful of cricket*. New York: Holt, Rinehart & Winston.	POETRY. A boy takes his pet cricket to school where it first disturbs the class with its chirping, but then becomes the show and tell attraction!
Cole, J. (1996). *The magic school bus: Inside a beehive*. New York: Scholastic.	LITERATURE. Miss Fissle takes her class on a field trip to a beehive on her magic school bus. (Great for creative writing)
Dallinger, J. (1981). *Lifecycle of a grasshopper*. Minnesota: Lerner.	SCIENCE. Lifecycle facts and good sources for illustrations, habitat, and creative writing.
Fackland, M. (1994). *The big bug book*. Boston: Little, Brown.	SCIENCE. Illustrations in this book are life size! Describes 13 of the world's largest insects, including the birdwig butterfly and the Goliath beetle.
Hoberman, M. A. (1998). *The llama who had no pajama: 100 favorite poems*. San Diego: Harcourt Brace.	POETRY and ART. This book contains several examples of traditional and contemporary poems about insects, animals, and natural themes.
Hopkins, L. B. (1992). *Flit, Flutter, Fly*. New York: Doubleday.	POETRY. Find wonderful poetry about insects in this poetry collection. This book is a great collection of "bug" poetry to dramatize with your class through drama, music, and movement. Add visual art by children.

Reference	Summary
Hornblow, L., & Hornblow, A. (1968). *Insects do the strangest things*. New York: Random House.	SCIENCE. Describes multiple insects that have peculiar and strange characteristics like the camouflage of the walking stick, the driver ants that prefer people to prunes, and the bugs that row themselves like boats on the water's surface.
Johnson, S. (1984). *Wasps*. Minnesota: Lerner.	SCIENCE. Describes wasp development and life style.
Kherdian, D. (1982). *The song of the walnut grove*. New York: Knopf.	LITERATURE. The adventures of a young cricket who finds friendship.
Koch, K., & Farrell, K. (1985). *Talking to the sun: An illustrated anthology of poems for young people*. New York: The Metropolitan Museum of Art.	ART. Outstanding collection of diverse poetry and great works of art from around the world. Several of the selections relate to insects and wildlife.
Laughlin, R. K. (1996). *Backyard bugs*. New York: Chronical Books.	SCIENCE. This book has GREAT full-color photos of 65 different bugs, including many insects. Fascinating background information tells about each creature.
Oxford Scientific Films. (1977). *Bees and honey*. New York: Putnam.	SCIENCE. Describes what goes on in a beehive. Great pictures up close!
Oxford Scientific Films. (1977). *The butterfly cycle*. New York: Putnam.	SCIENCE. Text and photographs follow the life cycle of a butterfly from egg through larva and pupa stages to adulthood.
Pinto, R. (1967). *The cricket winter*. New York: W.W. Norton.	LITERATURE. A little boy exchanges morse code messages with the cricket that lives in his house and together they trap the rat that has been plaguing the boy's father and the cricket's friends.
Schecter, D. (1997). *Science art: Projects and activities that teach science concepts and develop process skills*. New York: Scholastic.	ART, SCIENCE, and LITERATURE. Easy to follow activity links to national science standards. Literature links, art projects, poetry, journal suggestions, and patterns are all included in this book.

Table 4.6.   Curricular Connections Sources of Information: Insect Themes (continued)

Reference	Summary
Selsam, M.E. (1982). *Where do they go? Insects in winter.* New York: Four Winds.	SCIENCE. Explains how some insects fly south for the winter and others spend the cold months underground, under water, in unused buildings, or as eggs or pupae. Good for study of habitat, ecology, and for creating environments for art projects and drama.
Winslow, N. P., & Wright, J.R. (1987). *Bugs.* New York: Greenwillow.	POETRY. Labeled diagrams accompany soft illustrations of 16 different bugs. Humorous riddles complement the informative text.
Nuridsany, C., & Perennou, M. (1996). *MicroCosmos.* Hollywood, Calif.: Miramax Films.	VIDEO: SCIENCE/MUSIC. This 75-minute video was the winner of the Special Jury Prize, 1996 Cannes Film Festival. It captures the fun and adventure of a spectacular hidden universe revealed in a breathtaking, close-up view unlike anything you've ever seen. With its tiny cast of thousands, MicroCosmos leaves no doubt that Mother Nature remains the greatest special effects wizard of all.

You could ask the children, "What pictures of insects or habitats do see in your mind as you listen? Draw them silently or write about them as we listen." Ask the students to share those ideas (i.e., "I hear buzzing, gradually getting faster"). Discuss how the composer created the sounds, string instruments buzzed the bee sounds, or wooden percussion was used for the hopping segments. Outline what is happening in the music. Play the music again. Save the students' visual art and written responses to the music.

Poetry/Movement/Drama/Visual Arts? Reading Connections

Insect themes are also used in poetry. Find some insect poetry and have several members of the class read the poetry out loud (see table 4.6). Ask the students to read expressively, modeling how to do so with your own voice. Have the students say what they think about the poetry. "Which poems did you like? Why? Dislike? Why?" List their responses.

Students can illustrate their favorite poems or work cooperatively in groups to create movement tableaus (forming shapes with bodies, freezing, making new shapes) as selected insect poetry is read by others in the group. Ask the students to perform movements that make the poetry come alive, using their bodies as the poem's artwork. Ideas could be shared and performed, or saved.

Joyful Noise Activities

At this point, the teacher is ready to introduce the target book, *Joyful Noise*. Let the students know that a very interesting work was written that can be used to involve the whole class in creating their own insect performance for others or for videotaping. Introduce *Joyful Noise* by using overhead transparencies, pointing to and helping students follow the text. Students could do this initial reading in two groups. It is helpful to have the children on the left side of the room (as they look at the overhead) read the left column of the poetry and those on the right side (as they look at the overhead) read the right. You might wish for the students to each have copies of the transparencies.

After this initial large group reading, write the names of the insects found within *Joyful Noise* on the board or on an overhead transparency (grasshoppers, water striders, mayflies, fireflies, book lice, moth, water boatmen, digger wasp, cicadas, honeybees, whirligig beetles, requiem [about the effects of a killer frost], house crickets, chrysalis). Ask the students if they know all these bugs. Decide which insects are not well known and establish research teams to explore. Assign students to find information in science sources about the lesser-known insect characters and report back to the group.

Before reading out loud a second time, have the students carefully study *Joyful Noise*'s marvelous illustrations, read each poem's overhead silently, imagining the two voices (Have them mouth the words as they read silently). Explain again who will be reading which column. (The teacher may read one side of the page, students the other until the students are able to follow the direction and sequence of the poems' columns.) Stress expressive speech, let the students know the speed and volume you feel might be appropriate and why, or ask for their input. Read aloud again, exchanging parts or sides of the pages. Follow this pattern of silent reading, reading aloud, and rereading. Discuss each poem after the second reading, or discuss the entire work after all poems are read.

Discussion questions could include: "Which was your favorite poem? Why? What part did you like? Why? What did it mean to you? What did the poem tell us about the character? What do we still not know about the insects?" Students could write their responses in their developing bug journals.

Creating Performance Ideas for *Joyful Noise*

You and your students might want to further develop their artistic explorations of insect themes by actually performing *Joyful Noise* for others. When any poem is practiced as an "out loud" potential performance piece for others, children simply experience more chances to use
the poet's language with expression, movement, and drama.

Tell your students, "I wonder how we could turn *Joyful Noise* into a
performance with music, movement, art, acting, maybe some scenery
and lighting?" Take ideas, any ideas. Model one idea for staging a
poem: "I think we could use the Mannheim Steamroller 'Cricket'
recording (see the music sources in table 4.4) and create movement
right after we read the 'House Cricket' section of *Joyful Noise*. Any-
body have another idea?" List all ideas, no matter how unique; encourage appropriate choices—ideas that the children could actually accomplish during class sessions.

Ask the students, or draw names, to divide into the poem's insect
section groups (perhaps seven on one day, the last seven on the next).
Give the children an assignment to create a rather simple idea (not re-
quiring complex technology or laser shows!) to stage their group's
poem. Be sure that they know they will later be performing their ideas.
Let them loose, give them pep talks by visiting each group, or signal
the group if noise or motivation/behavior needs adjusting. Extend this
activity into another class session.

After the groups have decided on the staging of their insect poem
within *Joyful Noise,* have them share their rough idea, not the actual
staging, with the entire group. Let the students list an outline of action on the board (or blank overheads) for what will happen during
their performance. Let other students comment on the other groups'
ideas. Suggest ideas and encourage all groups. Allow one class session for group rehearsal. *It is paramount that the students "own"
their own stagings and that they are not re-creations of the teachers'
ideas about the meaning of the poetry.*

On another day, re-read the poems in sequence (without group
stagings) without stopping. Remind the students of expression,
speed, volume, and mood of each poem before starting the choral
reading rehearsal. Have each group decide who will be reading their
scene and how it will be read. Tell them to rehearse for a short time,
indicating where the action of their insect section will take place in
the room.

Frame or outline the whole production on a board where the students can see where they are in the book and who is next. Give the students copies of the entire work so that they can follow along, or use overheads. Let each group perform their interpretation of their insect section in the order presented in *Joyful Noise*. Have students make positive suggestions.

On another day, perform the entire work without stopping. Discuss, reward, and critique. Have a bug party!

Arrange to perform the work for another class or for videotaping. For this final performance, "insert" some paragraphs (to be read by the student authors) that were extracted from the student's initial writing about the *Joyful Noise* insects. Have the authors of these bug journal paragraphs read their statements right before the poem about that insect. For instance, before the poem, "House Crickets," a student reads "We had about a billion crickets in our house last August. My mother had to get some earplugs and we had to make the cats stay outside all night long. What a pain!" The insertion of the students' own impressions will make a creative, connective narrative full of humor and wry commentary that can only be created by young students.

The student drawings, journals, and examples of artwork could be displayed at the performance or scanned (filmed) by the video camera with voice-over narration. Classes could entitle the production, "Our *Joyful Noise*."

CONCLUSION

We encourage you to enjoy the creative processes that naturally evolve out of this kind of innovative, experience-based teaching of poetry. Whatever the outcome, you will have created expressive avenues of discovery about the poetry through multiple learning approaches in several curriculum areas. Simply put, you have taught in a manner that could reach more kids in more ways than simply blandly reading texts and assigning new vocabulary! Instead, you have set the scene for the children to make meaning about their experiences and how those experiences are reflected in books all around them. As Berghoff (2001) notes:

> Our curricula also need to take students to the aesthetic end of the continuum as often as possible because "lived" experiences are integrative experiences. As learners, we come to know more fully when our emotions and imaginations are stimulated. (p. 37)

Using activities like these, you have set the scene for the children to extract real meanings about the poetry through direct experience. What children learn with joy, they do not forget:

> When someone enjoys a wonderful painting, a beautiful building, or a good poem, he has begun to understand it. If he doesn't enjoy it, he might never understand it. With poetry, as with the other arts, pleasure leads to- and is a part of understanding. The best way to help young people to get something from poetry is to encourage them to like whatever they seem naturally to like, perhaps also expressing one's own enjoyment, thoughts, and enthusiasm. (Koch and Farrell, 1985, p. 106)

Questions for further discussion, study, and project development:

- How can we teach poetry that creatively and actively involves students in meaning making?
- In the haiku example, what are some of the ways that the students become actively engaged in arts activities? How does this engagement aid their oral language and literacy development?
- How is science instruction integrated into the *Joyful Noise* unit? And how are each of the four arts used within the context of this unit?
- Why are performances of learning within integrated arts units so vital to students' motivation and success?

CHAPTER 5

But What about the Other Subjects (Math, Science, and Social Studies)?

To live a creative life, we must lose our fear of being wrong.

—Joseph C. Pearce

HOW CAN I USE THE ARTS TO ENHANCE MY STUDENTS' UNDERSTANDING IN THESE SUBJECT AREAS?

As students get older, the content within their school subjects becomes more dense and oftentimes more difficult. As teachers, we attempt to provide quality instruction, not only in language arts, but also in math, science, social studies, and the arts. Naturally, our approach to content instruction involves interdisciplinary or integrated instruction. As noted in chapter 2, integrated instruction allows students to make connections between and among the disciplines and to grasp the information in such a way that they use it in new situations—our ultimate criteria!

Research on content instruction and comprehension suggests that students have a difficult time with text structures and understanding how the text they are reading is connected to other texts and information sources (e.g., Flood, Lapp, and Fisher, in press). In addition to direct comprehension instruction, *intertextuality* and *intermediality* have been suggested as aides to understanding content (e.g., Cairney, 1996; Lapp, Flood, and Fisher, 1999). *Intertextuality* refers to the unique connections that students make between the text they are currently reading and other texts that they have read. *Intermediality* suggests that readers also make connections between texts and other forms of media, including fine art, songs and musical listening, conversations, videos, performances of dance and theatre, etc. Taken together, intertextuality and intermediality are powerful learning supports that help students make otherwise obscure content meaningful, familiar, and understandable.

In order for teachers to make decisions and create purposeful integrated curriculum for student learning, they might need to first focus on two important considerations. First, what are some appropriate topical and conceptual instructional themes used within the grade level and/or discipline that are ripe for connections, correlations, and integration of student learning within and across multiple subject areas (see chapter 2)? Second, after appropriate themes for this teaching have been chosen, which content standards (including standards in the arts—see chapter 1) will be covered? These two important questions must first be addressed and, when carefully answered, will be at the heart of planning and implementing effective, purposeful, and successful integrated instruction.

The remainder of this chapter provides examples of integrated curriculum in specific content areas, including math, science, and social studies. Each of these sample thematic lessons provides readers with examples of intertextuality, intermediality, and arts integration within other subject areas. We believe that these three concepts are foundational to students' comprehensive understanding of the curriculum content and provide a breadth of opportunities toward the development of arts-loving readers.

TEACHING MATH CONTENT WITH INTEGRATED ARTS: TANGRAMS

When planning a recent mathematics unit for his class, Mr. Juarez utilized the mathematics standards designed by the National Council for Teachers of Mathematics (NCTM, 2000), as well as his state's content standards in other subjects (language arts and the arts). These documents were helpful when he mapped the year's thematic units with his colleagues. Mr. Juarez and his grade-level colleagues designed a thematic unit based on these geometry standards. As they did so, they considered various connections, correlations, and integration for this instruction, which would actively use social studies, the arts, and reading/language arts concepts articulated within the standards of those subject areas.

These educators were inspired by a problem at their new school building (Frey, in press). Construction delays had left a large central courtyard unpaved when school opened. The teachers obtained permission to incorporate small tile patterns into the final design of the courtyard and were determined to actually use the students' work within the courtyard design. Therefore, one of the outcomes for their thematic unit was the creation of student tile designs for use in the school courtyard project. In the unit "The Geometry Around Us," the students would also:

- classify, compare, and sort geometric figures.
- understand basic concepts of spatial relationships, symmetry, and reflections.
- use objects to perform geometric transformations.
- write simple informational text.
- apply the concepts of distance, scale, and relative location.
- speak publicly in a small group presentation.

Because one of the outcomes of this unit was to create a work of art, Mr. Juarez also wanted students to understand meanings and relationships between their unit work and concepts used in the arts. He wanted students to actively participate in learning about "Geometry Around Us" through direct activity in the arts so that students would be able to make more meaningful connections between their learning in mathematics, other subjects, and the real world. Additionally, the students would be led to evaluate their art activities and experiences as connections were made between these activities and other learning at hand. The arts standards contained within this integrated unit included the following (see chapter 1):

Visual Art:

- Understanding and applying media, techniques, and processes
- Using knowledge of structures and functions
- Choosing and evaluating a range of subject matter, symbols, and ideas

Drama:

- Script writing by planning and recording improvisations based on personal experience and heritage, imagination, literature, and history
- Designing by visualizing and arranging environments for classroom dramatizations

Music:

- Improvising melodies, variations, and accompaniments
- Composing and arranging music within specified guidelines

Dance:

- Identifying and demonstrating movement elements and skills in performing dance
- Understanding dance as a way to create and communicate meaning

Once the specific standards and expectations had been identified, Mr. Juarez followed a four-step process for designing the thematic unit. The four elements of standards-based lesson design include identifying:

1. books, materials, and other information sources.
2. instructional arrangements.
3. projects and class activities.
4. assessments and final products (Fisher and Frey, in press). This is one of many processes available to teachers to design curriculum units.

Step 1: Books, Materials, and Information Sources

Because the unit would involve tangrams (a Chinese puzzle consisting of a square cut into seven shapes, used to create other figures) and tessellations (mosaic patterns created by geometric shapes), Mr. Juarez knew that he would need enough sets of shapes to accommodate all of the learners in his class. He also wanted his students to experience lots of examples of tangrams and tessellations, beyond those offered in the math textbook. He supplemented his classroom library with children's literature on these topics. New additions to the library included *Grandfather Tang's Story* (Tompert, 1997), *The Greedy Triangle* (Burns, 1995), *Patterns* (Bulloch, 1994), *Reflections* (Jonas, 1987), *Shapes, Shapes, Shapes* (Hoban 1986), and *The Seasons Sewn: A Year in Patchwork* (Paul, 1996). These titles represented a range of reading levels, from the nearly wordless Hoban book to the more complex *The Greedy Triangle*. Thus, he could ensure that all his students would have access to informational text at an independent level. He also bookmarked math Web sites featuring pattern puzzles on his classroom computers for students to use during learning centers and collected posters featuring patterns and mosaics.

Step 2: Instructional Arrangements

Once Mr. Juarez had listed his books and information sources, it was time to consider the instructional arrangements. To provide his students with a variety of opportunities to work with one another, he used large-group demonstrations for instruction, small-group assignments for exploration, cooperative group work for projects and performances, student-teacher conferences, and individual work. He believes that this allows each child to understand themselves as learners, as well as to appreciate the contributions from each member of the class. He mapped out the ten-day unit, then wrote daily interrelated lesson plans. On day two, for example, he introduced tangrams to the whole class in a shared reading of *Grandfather Tang's Story* (Tombert, 1997). This story of a grandparent entertaining his young granddaughter with an adventure tale told in tangrams was an ideal method for manipulating the shapes. Later, the book and shapes were placed in a learning center so that small groups could try to duplicate the patterns. Students were also placed in cooperative project groups. These cooperative groups would construct a poster of their tessellation design for the courtyard and present it to the class. Students also kept individual math journals of patterns they had constructed, accompanied by their written explanations of the processes they had used to create them. Mr. Juarez used these journals in the conferences he scheduled with each student.

Step 3: Projects and Class Activities

Mr. Juarez knows that student learning is enhanced when projects and activities are designed to give further experience in applying new concepts. He also finds these activities are helpful in gauging how each student is progressing in his or her learning. He spaced these projects and activities throughout the unit so that he could reteach, as necessary, any concepts that seemed unclear to his students.

In an initial arts-connection activity, for instance, the students were asked to individually create various shape designs with their bodies, responding to word cards denoting various geometric shapes (rectangle, triangle, square, etc.). Mr. Juarez structured this exploratory movement extension activity by using a simple musical sound cue (triangle, no pun intended!) to denote the beginning and end of each geometric shape-making process. The students were asked to remember their shapes and then create a movement sequence based on those geometric shapes. After the students had actively individually experimented with shapes, they were asked to work in cooperative groups to formulate and perform a group-movement pattern design for each of the shapes and end with a group design featuring multiple shapes in a mosaic arrangement. The students were encouraged to experiment with different designs and make decisions together about their final performance forms.

After an in-class performance sharing of group-movement ideas, Mr. Juarez then discussed with the students the processes of making and creating geometric shape designs. He invited the students to share their insights about what was interesting about each group's movement ideas. The students discovered that there were a variety of ways to arrange their bodies in these geometric shapes and designs. Furthermore, the students pointed out that variations of these designs also occur throughout patterns in the design of the classroom, local architecture, fabric in their clothing, and in fine art examples hung on the classroom walls. Mr. Juarez decided to make available several examples of the use of geometric shapes and patterns used within paintings, graphic arts, architecture, and fabric design. He was able to effectively take the next steps in his integrated approach by allowing for student input and curiosity to guide his integrated instructional sequence.

On another day, after sharing several pieces of fine art involving geometric shapes (the work of the famous graphic artist Escher and others), Mr. Juarez then asked the students to work in their same movement groups to create a large, colored, cut-paper mosaic or quilt of geometric shapes. The students worked on cutting and designing several times before final design decisions were made. The cut-paper medium allowed students to easily arrange and rearrange their group's design based on their shared discussion, spirited debate, and decision making. The students were asked to decide and experiment with creating an expressive and aesthetically pleasing arrangement of geometric shapes.

After their artwork was created, groups were invited to share their work with the class in a variety of ways. They were to title their artwork and create and perform a short musical composition using classroom percussion instruments (xylophones, metallophones, wooden and metal percussion, and drums) provided by the school music teacher. The students composed a short melody following the contours and shapes of the various geometric shapes within their art design. In addition, the students were encouraged to create a group poem or story line narration about their artwork. The groups were also asked to debrief with the class about their group art and decision-making processes and to field questions from the class members. After the class presentations, volunteer students offered to create a classroom mini-museum displaying group artwork, poems and story lines, as well as photos of the student artists in each group. On another day, the student group designs were placed on the floor to allow students to see the beginnings of possible ideas for the school courtyard design.

Mr. Juarez also gave students dot grid paper each day to complete assigned tessellation homework. They experimented with these mosaic patterns at home, then brought their ideas each day to their cooperative work groups, where they discussed the developing final designs. Each student also created a tangram puzzle and wrote a short story to explain the pattern. These puzzles were assembled into a class book and read in the math learning center.

Step 4: Assessments and Final Projects

Like all teachers, Mr. Juarez uses assessments and final products to assign grades and monitor student progress toward the state and district standards. Knowing that his students represented a range of talents and abilities, he assessed the various integrated projects and the tangram poster presentations by using a rubric. His quality-indicator rubric specified the basics of the assignment, possible enhancements, errors to avoid, and appearance. Although most of his students were assessed using this rubric, it allowed him to customize it to meet the needs of individual learners. Thus, each student was able to demonstrate his or her growth (see chapter 9 for information on assessments).

This description illustrates how math can be taught using processes of integration with arts and other subject areas. Our next unit provides an example of integrated science instruction that is organized in a chronological, sequential manner. Although the next unit plan differs from the math unit in format, it, too, contains the same essential features of curriculum organization mentioned earlier in this chapter: materials, instructional arrangements, projects, and assessments surrounding the topical theme of the night sky.

TEACHING SCIENCE CONTENT WITH INTEGRATED ARTS: THE NIGHT SKY

Should a child's study of the night sky be focused solely on scientific knowledge? True, elementary-age students are fascinated to learn about moons, planets, and stars. They eagerly learn the names and character-istics of each member of our solar system; the scientific components re-quired in our core curriculum. Although much measurable learning oc-curs during these science activities, teachers are often concerned that students also need aesthetic and expressive learning opportunities at-tentive to the artistic, cultural, and metaphoric contexts of the night sky.

Toward these ends, our integrated unit about the night sky begins with an historical/cultural work of art—a translation of an ancient poem about starlight from natives of the American Northeast:

We who sing are the stars
We sing with our light
We are birds of fire
We fly through the sky
Our light is starlight
We sing on the road of spirits.
   —Native American, Passamaquoddy
   (In *Star Walk* edited by Seymour Simon, Morrow Publishers, 1995)

No one can disagree that the beauty of the preceding poem appeals to our visual, aural, and kinesthetic imaginations. However, many teachers want their students to understand both the scientific informa-tion about the night sky as well as the cultural importance that astron-omy has in civilization. To address these goals, they use multiple gen-res of children's literature, including informational texts, myths and folktales, poetry, music, and stories.

Such informational texts as *Solar System* by John Egan (Golden Books Publishing, 1999), *Stars and Galaxies: Looking Beyond the Solar System* by Miquel Perez and Maria Rius (Barrons Educational Series, 1998), and *The Young Astronomer* by Harry Ford (DK Publishing, 1998) provide students with detailed information about the scientific components re-quired in the core curriculum. These books provide students with an ef-ferent or fact-level understanding of such science standards as "students develop an understanding of changes in the sky" or "objects in the sky have observable locations and patterns of movement."

However, informational texts do not provide students with an aes-thetic understanding of the cultural and metaphoric contexts of stars. For example, these informational books probably do not inform stu-dents that stars have guided ships, provided comfort to lost travelers, and have had many a wish bestowed upon them. Literature, poems, mu-sic, and myths provide children with more than stories; they provide a perspective about the world. Although we do not recommend that teachers teach "the night sky" without science books or other nonnarrative sources, we are suggesting that lasting memories can be created when an integrated approach to the curriculum is undertaken. Table 5.1 contains a number of children's literature sources that can be used to ensure that children have transactions with text and a more aesthetic response to the curriculum (Rosenblatt, 1995). The remainder of this lesson is organized in a chronological plan. This plan differs from the math lesson in format, but contains the same essential features: materials, instructional arrangements, projects, and assessments.

Introducing the Night Sky

Introducing a new theme to students is always a challenge. Before breaking out the science textbooks to learn about the night sky, we suggest that teachers experiment with some of the following ideas:

- Ask students questions about what they already know and love about stars (e.g, Ogle, 1986) and make a list of the ideas, shared aloud.
- Ask students if there are things about stars that they would like to know.
- Begin a "star gazing" journal and sketchbook using a simplified star chart to help students locate constellations with their family (see table 5.1).
- Star shapes are used in artwork, crafts, cooking, and media (e.g., cookies, posters, CD inserts, etc.). Ask students to bring star-shaped items to class.

This suggested sequence of opening activities more fully engages young learners in the sights, sounds, feelings, textures, and meanings of stars. The remainder of this sample unit was taught over a two-week period. Some teachers might choose to focus on certain components of this unit, but others will find value in following the unit's sequential development.

Discovering the Night Sky

After exploring the prior knowledge of the students, we introduced a book with many more rhyming questions about stars. We then read

Table 5.1. "Night Sky" Selections

Genre	Reference	Description
Poetry	Bruchac, J. (1995). *The earth under sky bear's feet: Native American poems of the land.* New York: PaperStar, The Putnam Berkley Group.	An outstanding collection of poems about the land. Several of the poems focus on the night sky.
Narrative and Song	Carpenter, M. C. (1998). *Halley came to Jackson.* New York: Harper Collins.	The book and song tell a tale of a baby whose father shows her the Halley comet in 1910 and hopes that she lives long enough to see it again.
Narrative	Cordes, J. (1999). *The hope star.* Bookworld Services	A mother's message to her children about hope, wishing, and the will to believe.
Narrative	Crew, G. (1997). *Bright star.* Kane Miller Books.	Alicia meets the astronomer John Tebbut who discovered the "Great Comet" of 1861 and is invited to visit his observatory.
Informational Text	Ford, H. (1998). *The young astronomer.* New York: DK Publishing.	This book provides readers with experiments and tips on how to get started observing the wonders of the planets, stars, and moon.
Narrative	Friedersdorf, M. (1997). *Where do falling stars go?* Orlando, Fla.: Peaceful Village Publishing.	This book has imaginative, rhyming text about the places that falling stars might go.
Narrative	Gutierrez, D. (1997). *The night of the stars.* Kane/Miller Books.	This is the story of a man who does not like the darkness of night so he finds a way to bring some light to it.
Narrative	Hort, L. (1991). *How many stars in the sky?* Tambourine.	A heart-warming story about a young boy who can't sleep and tries to count the stars.
Poetry	Hughes, L. (1994). *The dream keeper and other poems.* New York: Alfred Knopf.	A collection of poems about hopes, dreams, aspirations, life, and love in the sky.
Myth and Folktales	Kusugak, M. A. (1993). *Northern lights: The soccer trails.* Toronto: Annick Press.	In this Inuit tale of the northern lights, ancestors are playing soccer.
Myth and Folktales	Mayo, G. (1987, 1990). *Star tales* and *more star tales.* Walker.	These books are a collection of North American Indian stories of the night sky.

Genre	Reference	Description
Myth and Folktales	Oughton, J. (1992). *How the stars fell into the sky: A Navajo legend*. Boston: Houghton Mifflin Company.	The placement of the stars in the sky are explained in this text.
Poetry	Peter Pauper Press. (1960). *Cherry-blossoms: Japanese haiku, series three*. Mount Vernon, N.Y.: The Peter Pauper Press.	A collection of haiku poems from the great Japanese masters, including references to the night sky.
Narrative	Proimos, J. (1998). *Joe's wish*. New York: Harcourt Brace.	An old man who wishes on a star to be young again, until he spends the day with his grandson. Students will love the cartoons.
Historical Fiction	Ringold, F. (1992). *Aunt Harriet's underground railroad in the sky*. New York: Crown Books.	This book tells of the escape from slavery and how people might have met Harriet Tubman.
Poetry	Siegen-Smith, N. (1999). *A pocket of stars: Poems about the night*. Barefoot Books.	The night sky is illuminated through this book's rich collection of poems.
Poetry and Visual Art	Simon, S. (1995). (Ed.) *Star walk*. New York: William Morrow.	For older students, this book contains outstanding photography, famous quotations, and wonderful poetry about stars and space.
Informational	Thompson, C.E. (1989). *Glow in the dark constellations: A field guide for young stargazers*. New York: Grosset and Dunlap.	A handy beginner's guide to stargazing, including glow-in-the-dark constellations, instructions for locating star groups, legends, and sky maps.
Narrative	Winter, J. (1988). *Follow the drinking gourd*. New York: Alfred Knopf.	This is a story of escaping slaves and how they used the Big Dipper as a navigation system.

After each verse, we asked the children to reach for that star, think of their wish, and bring it close to their heart—with their eyes closed. We asked the students to remember their wishes, but to keep the wishes to themselves. When all three verses had been sung, we asked the children to return to their desks, where they found three large blank star cut-outs. The students then wrote out one wish per paper star. We reminded them not to put their names on the papers because wishes are secret.

We extended the student's star wish writing by creating a bulletin board, where the students attached their star wishes throughout the day. Our second grade students asked for many additional paper stars to write more wishes for the bulletin board display. Enrique wrote "I wish I was always good" while Kumasi wrote "I wish that my grandmother would get her new wheelchair." Older students added star wishes to their journal writing and were very reflective of the difficulty in making wishes come true. For example, as part of one of Gabrielle's entries, she wrote "Wishing keeps me focused, but I know how hard it is to make things happen. My parents are fighting a lot and I wish my house was calmer."

Star Journal

Throughout this unit, students continued their collection of observations, thoughts, and illustrations in a scrapbook fashion, reflecting their experiences of the unit. We used daily open-ended writing prompts that students responded to, including: "Last night when I looked at the stars, I imagined . . . " or "Tomorrow when I star gaze, I hope : . ." or "Once upon a time, someone looked up to the stars and . . ."

Legends

Now that the students had been introduced to the personal imaginative meanings of stars, it was natural to tell them that many people, all over the world, have been looking at stars just like they have been. We used an authentic Navajo legend about how the stars were placed in the sky, *How the Stars Fell Into the Sky: A Navajo Legend* (Oughton, 1992). This was an excellent choice for our read-aloud and a creative dramatic performance piece in which children designed simple sets and props to retell the legend.

The book *Tales of the Shimmering Sky: Ten Global Folktales With Activities* (Milord, 1996) features many short legends, art activities, science projects, and interesting facts about stars. Two particularly evocative legends are "Great Bear: A Tale from the Micmac Indians of Eastern Canada" and "The Boastful Star: A Tale from Polynesia." In Great Bear, students are introduced to the Big Dipper through a legend about a bear who is chased throughout the year by small birds as an explanation for the changing position of stars. The Boastful Star focuses on a smaller constellation, known as Pleiades, also known as "seven sisters" by the ancient Greeks, which looks like a smaller version of the Big Dipper. The book offers several legends and explanations of this small constellation. Our older students scripted these tales into performance pieces accompanied by their own musical compositions performed on Orff instruments (xylophones, metallophones) and assorted classroom percussion instruments. Our younger students enjoyed the performances by their older peers.

In addition, many students were intrigued with the concept of the northern lights in Alaska. An Inuit legend, written about in *Northern Lights: The Soccer Trails* (Kusugak, 1993), provided a mythical explanation about this phenomenon. The legend explains the northern lights as a playing field on which Inuit ancestors are playing a game of soccer. Several of the boys picked out figures of soccer players within the book's illustrations. The after-school soccer coach told us about the conversations that students were having about stars during their soccer game—clearly our curriculum was transcending the school day.

Oh, Watch the Stars

A number of literature selections deal with the concept of counting the stars in the sky (see table 5.1). *How Many Stars in the Sky?* (Hort, 1991) is an African American story about a boy who can't sleep and decides to count the stars. His father takes him from the city to the country, where he can really see the night sky. This read-aloud was a natural lead-in to a Southern folk tune "Oh, Watch the Stars" (see table 5.2). During the instrumental ending of this recording, the children dramatized how they could count the stars and fall asleep under the open sky.

Once this quiet mood was established, the children enjoyed Mary Chapin Carpenter's recorded song and accompanying book of song text, *Halley Came to Jackson* (1998). The book and cassette are a rendition of a story about the visit of Halley's comet to Jackson, Mississippi in 1910. The baby in the story grows up to be an older woman who sees the comet again in 1986. After listening to the song, the students were asked to respond to the journal prompt, "What will you be doing the next time Halley's comet travels by?" Cory wrote that he hoped to be an airline pilot flying by as the comet soared. Jennifer wrote that she would be reading books to her grandson. Marshawn wrote that he would be living on another planet and would miss it.

Activities for Learning Centers

Learning centers are a great way to cover material, allow cooperative groups, and personalize instruction. However, before our students began work at the centers, we modeled behavior, procedures for completing tasks, and the various outcomes we expected. We created one center rotation on poetry (see table 5.1). Students at this center could select a poem, read it, and then illustrate their understanding of the poem.

Another center was devoted to having students create a musical composition based on the outline shapes of simple star constellations. We provided the students with patterns of stars and asked them to connect these patterns with dotted pencil lines into a shape. The students then experimented, creating a melody on barred instruments (xylophone, tone bells), which followed the up and down and short and long outlines of their created constellation shape. Students wrote a journal entry about their constellation composition. These compositions were performed for the whole class.

Another center focused on science art projects, such as making starry constellation viewers, starry sky bookmarks, and 3-D constellations made from marshmallows and toothpicks (e.g., Schecter, 1997). We also used some of the art projects from *Tales of the Shimmering Sky: Ten Global Folktales With Activities* (Milord, 1996). One last center provided students the opportunity to search the Internet for information about stars, sites to watch stars, and places to interact with other stargazers.

Culminating Activity: "Festival of the Night Sky"

Although integrated curriculum units of this nature need not always be thought of in terms of "product value through performance," this particular unit is a naturally informal combination of sharing of children's journals, artwork, songs, movement activities, and original music compositions. A night sky background was created to display and perform the student's work. Several other classes from the same grade level or younger were invited as an audience during the school day to view our performance. We created a story line narration that introduced the various works that students created during this unit. After our "Festival of the Night Sky," several teachers requested books, poetry, song recordings, and other materials for use in their own classrooms. Several parents attended the festival and asked for a list of the books we used so that they could purchase them for their children. Plans have been made to collaboratively design new integrated arts lessons, such as transportation, Westward expansion, dinosaurs, and ancient civilizations.

TEACHING SOCIAL STUDIES CONTENT WITH INTEGRATED ARTS: HOPE AND FREEDOM

Ms. Wally was her grade-level representative on her school-site social studies curriculum team. This team of teachers decided to formulate a curriculum in which various grade levels could contribute toward a common school-wide instructional outcome—a shared integrated arts performance about student learning within a conceptual social studies curriculum theme—stemming from classroom activities featuring the integration of social studies with music, language arts, and drama. After lengthy discussions and teacher brainstorming sessions, the social studies team decided to focus on a conceptual theme that the whole school could embrace. However, their idea for this theme was very broad and presented special challenges for the unit planners.

The teachers wanted to focus on historical events and peoples' real-life experiences within the time progression in African American history—from slavery, to emancipation, the struggle for civil rights, to today's concerns for the hope and freedom of all people. After consulting their state social studies content standards as well as frameworks and standards in the visual and performing arts, Ms. Wally and her colleagues considered various theme titles for this unit and finally decided on the concept theme, "Hope and Freedom." Within this broader focus, they hoped various grade levels could participate (in age-appropriate ways) in a culminating, thematic integrated arts performance of songs, narration, poetry, drama (scripted short plays), student journals, and artwork about "Hope and Freedom."

The planning team also decided that the concept of "Hope and Freedom" should not be exclusively relegated to activities that only occur during Black History Month, but rather that this important curriculum theme rightly deserved continual focus and should be experienced by their students throughout the year. Many teachers felt the students in their school needed many expressive/artistic outlets for their emotional reactions to traumatic current events, home, neighborhood and school issues, and events continually discussed in the media. The children in Ms. Wally's school were not unaware of the world around them. In fact, they were keenly aware of very real problems in their everyday lives. The teachers talked about important concepts for student learning about hope and freedom, including the following: respect, hope, civil rights, freedom from discrimination and acts of hatred and violence, and intolerance of differences in religion, ethnicity, appearance, as well as psychological and physical differences among people. The team felt their future school-wide performance needed a story line or organizing thought statement to guide the teachers in their integrated instruction toward expressive student outcomes. One teacher wrote:

> This is the story, a journey through words and song, of the African American struggle for freedom—from the experiences of slavery, to the Great Emancipation, the beginnings of freedom, to the lofty thoughts and poetic dreams of a great leader, Dr. Martin Luther King, to the voices of today's children. It speaks of all our continuing hopes for freedom, acceptance, and celebration of difference, color, religion and all that separates us from our fellow human beings.

Team members created a poster of this statement for each teacher at the school site. Other teachers in the school were then asked to team with social studies team members to formulate materials and information sources, decide on instructional arrangements, create and lead (team teaching) projects and activities, and prepare for the unit's authentic assessment—a school-wide integrated arts performance and ensuing evaluations.

Step 1: Books, Materials, and Information Sources

Because the unit would involve songs and chants, famous speeches, and poetry about the "Hope and Freedom" theme, the teachers began their search for appropriate materials. They began to collect informational books, children's literature, songs and CD recordings, videotapes, and photojournalism about the period. They asked each teacher for ideas they might already be using in the classroom and asked those teachers to share their materials and lesson ideas with others. The librarian/media technician offered the book *Martin's Big Words* by Doreen Rappaport (2001). A third grade teacher shared the book *My Dream of Martin Luther King* by Faith Ringgold (1998) and a fifth grade teacher shared a chapter book *The Life and Words of Martin Luther King Jr.* by Ira Peck (2000).

The teachers also wanted students to learn a variety of songs, including echo songs (call and response), traditional African American spirituals about freedom themes, updated rap-style compositions using appropriate song texts based on the "Hope and Freedom" theme, and traditional American patriotic songs. An adopted state series in music provided many song selections, lesson ideas and extensions, and accompanying CD recordings appropriate for their needs (see table 5.3). Among the selected songs were, "Ev'rybody Ought to Know" (call and response for younger children) recorded by the group Sweet Honey in the Rock, "Oh, Freedom" (traditional spiritual), "Martin Luther King Rap" (rhythmic speech and body percussion for older children), and a gospel rendition of "America" ("Oh beautiful for spacious skies . . .").

Each of these song melodies and song text appeared within adopted state series student books and on accompanying CD recordings designed to help the teachers teach the students the song. In addition, the state series provided CD recordings of famous artists performing African American songs of hope and freedom, including performances by Odetta, the Harlem Boys Choir, Sweet Honey in the Rock, and others. The teachers wanted to use these recordings for musical listening and response. Finally, the same state text offered excellent poetry about the era: "Martin Luther King Day" by Myra Cohn Livingston and the African American Freedom Anthem text, "Lift Every Voice" by James Weldon Johnson.

The teachers wanted to utilize quality poetry within the school-wide performance. One teacher suggested two poems for reading and student projects: "My People" and "Dreams" from *The Dream Keeper and Other Poems* by the great African American poet Langston Hughes (1994). Both

Table 5.3. Resources for Hope and Freedom

Title	The Music Connection Grade, TE pg, CD #	Making Music Grade, TE pg, CD #
"Ev'rybody Ought to Know"	1, pg. 240, CD 6–39	
Poem: "Martin Luther King Day"	1, pg. 241	7, pg. 263
"Oh Freedom"	5, pg. 199, CD 8–21–23	5, pg. 380, CD 15–15
"Martin Luther King Chant"	4, pg. 198, CD 8–11	
Poem: "Lift Ev'ry Voice and Sing"	4, pg. 59	
"Lift Ev'ry Voice and Sing"		5, pg. 466, CD 18–6
"America" (gospel version)	5. Pg. 225, CD 9–24	
"We Shall Overcome"		5, pg. 466, CD 18–10

of these poems express the desire for respect, peace, and the pursuit of dreams and freedom. Another teacher suggested using part of Abraham Lincoln's *Gettysburg Address* (1863) paired with a section of Dr. Martin Luther King Jr.'s "I Have a Dream" speech delivered in 1963 (100 years later) at the steps of the Lincoln Memorial during the historic March on Washington. The teachers felt selections from these two speeches could be supplemented with videos and photos of the Lincoln Memorial, Dr. King's televised speech, social studies text materials, and historical videos about the *Gettysburg Address*, *Emancipation Proclamation*, freedom marches, and the March on Washington. They hoped these resources might be a catalyst for student created scripts and biographical dramatizations of key events in this period.

Primary teachers wanted to explore the meanings of the words freedom, justice, friendship, and happiness. They made large, colored poster cards with these words written on them and used them for class discussions to pair with the song, "Ev'rybody Ought to Know." These teachers also needed to create large, illustrated word posters for song texts that were a challenge for the little ones to master.

Finally, the teachers sought to use quotes from the book, *Dear Dr. King: Letters from Today's Children to Dr. Martin Luther King, Jr.* (Colbert and Harms, 1998), a collection of contemporary Memphis schoolchildren's letters to the great civil rights leader. In this source, the children's letters are set within photos of the time. One teacher suggested that the book be used as a model for their school-wide collection of illustrated student letters to Dr. King.

Step 2: Instructional Arrangements and
Step 3: Projects and Class Activities

The planning team agreed that it was important for the teachers to create their own ideas and ways to deliver instruction within this integrated unit as they worked toward a school-wide performance in four weeks. The thought here was that teachers would be more likely to experiment with arts integration if allowed to pursue avenues of instruction in ways in which they feel most comfortable. For instance, four teachers decided to divide the responsibility of teaching the elements of this unit's instruction. One teacher offered to teach the song material, another led the children's letter writing to Dr. King, another led discussions and information about the historical period, while the last teacher designed opportunities for the children to write, script characters, rehearse, create backdrops and costumes, and perform dramatizations of their own stories about slaves, freedom fighters, and historical figures. In this way, no one teacher felt overburdened or without time and resources.

To provide students with a variety of ways to work with one another, large group demonstrations and rehearsals were used for song learning and musical listening; small group work was used for cooperative student script writing, and decision making about stage direction and dramatization, and individuals prepared narration and letters to Dr. King. Other small groups were assigned prop making, scenery, and lighting duties. The teachers believed that this variety of instructional arrangements allowed for heightened student creativity within individual classes and teamed, grade-level combinations. Each teacher agreed to do what was possible for their class toward the preparation of the school-wide program. All students were to learn the songs and write illustrated letters to Dr. King. Groups of older children participated in the narrations and dramatizations. All students would attend and participate in some way in the school-wide performance offered once during the school day and once in the early evening so that parents and others could attend. The performances were videotaped for students to debrief, evaluate, and discuss.

Individual teachers led other experiences and avenues for student learning including a "Hope and Freedom" mini-museum display of student artwork, bulletin board displays about famous African American and other freedom fighters, newspaper and magazine cut-paper collages about current events linked to issues of hope and freedom, clay busts and dioramas of great African Americans, and class novels about the imagined lives of slave children, freedom fighters and others. One class scripted their class novel and produced a twenty-five-minute theatre piece about the lives of Harriet Tubman and Rosa Parks. This play was co-sponsored and presented by the young students at a local university, with proceeds given toward integrated arts resources at the school site.

Step 4: Assessments and Final Projects

The social studies/integrated arts planning team solicited other teachers' input in designing an assessment of student learning within the "Hope and Freedom" performance unit. It was decided that students should: prepare songs, dramatizations, and letters; participate in the performances; and evaluate and critique those learning experiences. Because performances are authentic arts assessments of the learning, students were asked to view the videotape of the performance, write journal responses to facts and ideas they learned in the unit, think of and write about other things they would like to learn within the unit, and evaluate each group performance. In addition, each grade level developed a simple rubric for student evaluation of their own and others' efforts (see chapter 9).

The performance event was photographed and written up in the school and district newsletter. In addition, the principal, school board members, parents, and teachers were asked to evaluate the unit experiences and provide added feedback. The students, parents, and teachers were also asked to think of other school-wide themes. Finally, all involved heartily requested that teachers and students participate in one school-wide integrated arts theme performance per year and that these themes should be alternated between social studies, math, science, and language arts conceptual themes. By consensus, the theme for the next year's unit was "The Desert."

In conclusion, this chapter has richly explored a variety of instructional approaches, where children learn content in other subjects through expressive avenues provided in the arts. As part of our schools' core curriculum instruction in the arts, students not only learn about arts, artists, and their own art-making experience, but can also learn content in other subject areas with and through the arts. In this way, arts become a way of learning and knowing in all of our classrooms. These varied learning experiences can include creating, performing, analyzing, and evaluating arts integration activity within other subject matter. For all our children to develop as arts-loving readers, we must continue to explore ideas, planning resources, teaching strategies, and assessment and evaluation of arts within the general curriculum.

Questions for further discussion, study, and project development:

- How does integrated arts instruction increase student comprehension and learning?
- What two important questions must teachers ask themselves when developing integrated arts curriculum?

- Using the four-part curriculum development model provided in this chapter, develop your own integrated arts unit. As you develop this unit, consider the following questions:
- How have you addressed literacy development?
- Which content areas receive the most attention? Why?
- Which standards do you address in the content areas of science, social studies, arts, math, and language arts?
- How are each of these standards addressed in your lesson?
- What are some of the expected student learning outcomes from your lesson?
- How is performance incorporated into your lesson?

CHAPTER 6

How Do We Teach about Artists and Their Craft?

I shut my eyes in order to see.

—Paul Gauguin

The task of developing arts-loving readers can be a joyous pursuit. Rich contexts for learning about the arts are easily found within many children's books. Curiosity, imagination, and aesthetic understanding can be sparked through meaningful learning activities related to literature about the arts and the artists who make them. The underlying premise here is that children can learn a great deal about the arts and their own innate artistry through total involvement and immersion in the experiences in which they are invited to actively read, write, listen, move, respond, create, interact, and directly express ideas.

Previous chapters have focused on language arts, poetry, science, math, and social studies. This chapter provides teachers with ideas for using the arts as content and the focus of instruction. Of course, the ideas in this chapter complement both specialized and integrated arts educational opportunities that all students should have in the elementary and middle school.

To achieve these purposes, this chapter describes literature about the arts and offers practical teaching applications in which children can be actively engaged in developing and enhancing the following literacy skills:

- Searching, predicting, confirming, monitoring, and rereading
- Expanding vocabulary and applying concepts
- Making predictions and forming opinions about story content, characters, plot, theme, setting, etc.

- Defining and sequencing information to make or do a procedure (creative movement, illustrations, dramatizations, reports, performances, etc.)
- Asking questions, listening and contributing to discussions, using language cues to indicate understanding, and responding to and volunteering ideas in response to others' questions
- Working in groups to make decisions, brainstorm, and problem-solve as information and content is shaped to achieve a purpose (informal performance or display)

In addition, this chapter offers practical ideas for creative reader response activities linked to selected children's literature sources about the arts. The following concepts are integrated within suggested teaching applications toward creative reader response:

- Learning what it means to be an artist; where we find art; what artists, actors, and musicians do and know; and how we can be various types of artists, too.
- Learning to look at art, learning to listen to music, learning to move, dance, and create and portray characters, plot, and action.
- Building vocabulary and understanding about concepts and elements in music theatre, dance, and in visual art.
- Explorations of the lives and works of great painters, musical artists and composers, dancers and choreographers, actors and directors.
- Suggestions for creative response activity (visual art projects, creative drama projects, music making, musical listening, journal and other writing, choral reading, poetry, creative movement, and performance sharing) to children's literature about music, dance, visual art, and drama (theatre) of varying historical periods, genres, and diverse cultural origins.

Naturally, we have written this chapter with focus on the development of arts-loving readers through active learning applications, which utilize appropriate arts vocabulary, literature, creative and integrative performance opportunities, and activities designed to help students analyze and value various arts experiences. In these ways, our students' active, creative responses to literature about arts and artists is a key component toward the development of their love of reading through and with the arts. Following the list of children's books and appropriate teaching application suggestions surrounding the four arts (music, dance, theatre, and visual art) and their artists, we present a sample integrated arts lesson—this one focused on teaching students about string music, musicians, and instruments.

BACKGROUND FOR THE STUDY OF ARTS AND ARTISTS

Creative/expressive response to literature, sometimes reserved as an extra enrichment activity or belonging within the teaching realm of arts specialists with highly talented students, can instead be an important learning medium for many, if not all children. To this argument, Hancock (2000) adds:

> The ability to express oneself through dramatic presentation, artistic media, or musical prowess, however, is the preferred mode of response for many children. Integrating the expressive arts into the lives of all children through response to children's literature should be considered a natural part of the culture of childhood.
>
> Although the oral and written response to literature dominate research and practice in the area of literature-based instruction, the expressive modes of response offer endless possibilities for sharing personal response to children's books. (p. 254)

There are several other bonuses to using books about visual art, dance, theatre, and music as catalysts for creative reader response. Within students' active learning transactions with text, several curriculum areas may be naturally and effectively integrated, including the arts, language arts, social studies, science, and math (Jacobs, 1989, 1997; McDonald and Fisher, 1999a, 2000). Additionally, this kind of practical, purposeful curricular integration may offer needed assistance to classroom teachers who may have great desire, but limited background and time, to actively engage their students in learning about and within the arts (Barry, 1998). Finally, these kinds of valuable literature-based learning experiences for children might be shared with arts specialists in need of collaboration and support from classroom teachers as they develop teaching materials and strategies connecting the arts to the larger school curriculum (McDonald and Fisher, 2000) (see chapter 7). Now turn to children's books and teaching ideas organized into three areas, which serve to include all the arts. These sections include: visual art and artists, music and musicians, and creative movement and dance and dramatic response to literature.

BOOKS ABOUT VISUAL ART AND ARTISTS

Learning to Look at Art

Remember a moment when you personally have been taken in by the beauty of a particular painting? (The world stops for a few moments as you are happily immersed in the painting, completely focused in the act of purposeful looking.) What was it about that work that held your attention and interest? Was it the colors, the lines, the use of light, the subject? What did that art work mean to you? Can you still "see" that work of art in your mind? Can you tell us something about that painting? What do you think is happening in that painting? Show us how the colors move within the painting. These and other evocative questions and response prompts are important to consider as we seek to engage children in looking at art within varying contexts found in literature.

Many books offer an excellent variety of art as well as child-centered suggestions for engaging young readers into looking, thinking, discussing, and responding to visual art. In their engagement with the following literature, children are actively utilizing and developing a number of literacy skills:

Brown, R. (1982). *If at first you do not see.* **New York: Henry Holt.** Richly illustrated, delightful story of a wayward caterpillar who searches for something to eat. Things are never the way they might first appear. The reader first sees the book's upside-down paintings of the next scene in the story sequence, then must turn the book around to discover (and delight in) the illustration's link to the story plot.

Application: Use this book to help children develop visual literacy and attention to color, line, shape, and form as they read the text and manipulate the book's up or down direction.

Carle, E. (1992). *Draw me a star.* **New York: Philomel.** Simple, cumulative text set within the author/artist's bold illustrations. "Draw me a star . . . and the artist drew a star. It was a good star. . . . Draw me a sun, said the star. . . and the artist drew a sun. . . ." Young readers are treated to the highly imaginative, kinesthetic nature of the author's illustrations.

Application: Invite the students to create their own drawings and creative movement sequenced to this text. Also use for discussion, vocabulary building, and expressive group read-alouds.

Carle, E. (1984). *The mixed-up chameleon.* **New York: Harper-Collins.**
Whimsical, highly creative illustrated text (set in cumulative style) about a little chameleon who discovers his life would be a lot more interesting if he could change his color, shape, and size to be like the animals he sees at the zoo. However, he hadn't counted on becoming various parts of these animals all at once! Very funny results ensue within this natural story vehicle.

Application: Use within group read-alouds to focus attention not only to colors, but to shapes, designs, body parts, and animal names to your youngest readers. Create a word wall and simple art projects about the character and plot, and add creative movement to prompts from the story's action verbs, animal shapes, and body parts, and new vocabulary.

Collins, P. (1992). *I am an artist.* **Brookfield, Conn.: Millbrook Press.**
Each line of this sensitive, poetic text naturally immerses the reader into a directional, left to right viewing of the superbly illustrated, two-page, visual environment settings. The vocabulary-rich text and excellently paired illustrations emphasize that we are all artists whenever "we listen and search and see" as the words guide the reader in ways to do so.

Application: Children of all ages can be invited to look at the paintings first, then read aloud words on the page. Further activity could be to have children draw illustrations of certain sections of the text and display on classroom bulletin boards and original student art books. Older children could also work in pairs or small groups as they cover up the text: first looking, then reading text aloud, re-looking, and reading as they look. The text might also be scripted as a reader's theatre (everyone saying the reoccurring refrain, "I am an Artist," with small groups expressively speaking other sections "when . . ."). Additional ideas for this book include student-created movement sequences paired with recordings of nature sounds or discussions about how we all have opportunities to be artists in our everyday lives.

Lionni, L. (1995). *Matthew's dream.* **New York: Knopf.**
This is the tale of a little mouse and his friend's visit to an art museum. Later, the mouse dreams he and his friend are walking on (within) a huge painting and its changing colors and textures. Through these whimsical experiences, the characters decide to become painters, too!

Application: Use this book as an excellent introduction to a museum field trip or for focusing class discussions after looking at several pieces of art.

Wolfe, G. (1999). *Oxford first book of art.* **New York: Oxford University Press.**
This book is an incredible collection of paintings, drawings, sculptures, and textiles from many cultures and historical periods.
   Application: Use this book's suggestions for easy-to-follow, highly interactive, interesting, and stimulating discovery activities for classroom discussions, writing, drawing, and other creative responses.

WHAT IS ART? WHAT DO ARTISTS DO? CONCEPTS, ELEMENTS, AND TOOLS ARTISTS USE

Although many of us love great paintings and we might also know quite a bit about artists who painted them, the task of communicating our knowledge and love of that art can seem overwhelming. How do we invite children into discussions, discovery, and active experimentation with art, its elements, and vocabulary? What kinds of literature create contexts in which children can see the works of great artists within authentic biographies about their lives and works? The following books offer some answers:

dePaola, T. (1989). *The art lesson.* **New York: Putnam & Grosset.**
The story of a little first grade boy, Tommy, and his quest to become a professional artist when he grows up. His excitement is heightened as he hears he will be meeting his school art teacher. Tommy's disappointment ensues when the art teacher asks for students to merely copy her examples, rather than create their own art. However Tommy knows that all *real* artists create their own ideas for their art! Finally, a resolution to the problem is found and little Tommy's (the author) love of art remains, even today, unlimited and unfettered.
   Application: Read this book aloud. Engage the students in a group discussion about how we all have our own ways of making art and the value of those differences. Allow the children to individually display and comment on art they made as the class is encouraged to pay attention and praise others' efforts.

Gibbons, G. (2000). *The art box*. New York: Holiday House.
The book shows children in the process of making art and the supplies, procedures, and tools used.

Application: Use in read-alouds as a focus activity before and after children engage in individual art-making activities. This book contains a wonderful introduction to colors, tools, and supplies artists use to draw and paint. Stress the idea that we are all artists because we all make and love art.

Heller, R. (1995). *Color*. New York: Puffin Books.
The book's bold, brilliantly colored illustrations and rhythmic, poetic text gently lead readers to on-the-page discovery learning about colors, the color spectrum, paint color mixing, color variation, the processes of printmaking, shade, tint, and so much more. Visual art mediums featured in illustrations include pencil, markers, crayons, chalk, tube paints, graphics, and transparencies.

Application: Read this book aloud, or have children read in small groups, before and/or after their direct, hands-on art experimentation in color study (crayons, paint, markers, chalk, and other mediums). Use the text for building vocabulary about the elements of art and discussions of how we make art.

Karas, G. (2001). *The class artist*. New York: Greenwillow.
Young Fred has created wonderful, secret plans for his class art project. He takes his time creating his week-long project, so much so that the time has passed and he's hardly made a thing! After a lot of frustration and embarrassment, Fred enjoys a flurry of creative inspirations and ends up the hero of the class art projects. Young students will enjoy this humorous and charming story about how we learn to make our own art.

Application: Script and dramatize the text of this wonderful book. Pair performances with student made art displays incorporated as the scenery of the play about *The Class Artist*. Encourage older children to perform a dramatization of this book for younger students and allow time for cross-age read-alouds or shared reading of the book.

Rylant, C. (1988). *All I see*. New York: Orchard Books.
Set within a dreamlike setting, this is the story of a boy's (Charlie) developing awareness of art and artful seeing. Charlie experiences a new

friendship with a soon-to-be-mentor artist he meets by chance. Charmingly quiet, subdued water-colored illustrations help transport the reader into the seeing and feeling contexts of Charlie's curious imagination about the older Gregory's painting and art-making.

Application: After reading this book, use in group discussions of what artists do. Ask the students some of the following kinds of questions: How do artists see? What are they interested in? Why do artists like to paint outside? What kinds of scenes and subjects would you paint? Why? List the student's answers on a chart about artists and the work they do.

Lives and Works of Great Painters

Many books offer wonderful biographical contexts for understanding the lives and learning about the works of great painters. Others offer stories based on their lives, works, and times in which these great artists lived. Pair these books with multiple viewings and discussions of the art of these famous painters:

Vincent van Gogh

Anholt, L. (1994). *Camille and the sunflowers: A story about Vincent van Gogh.* **New York: Barrons.**
This story is based on the real-life encounter of a young boy named Camille with the artist Vincent van Gogh. The two become friends during their time spent in a Dutch country village. Delightful text and illustrations are based on van Gogh's painting style and works of this period.

Application: Use this story to pair with the reading of other books about van Gogh as well as with books showing his actual art works (see Resources for Teaching).

Isom, J. (1997). *The first starry night.* **Watertown, Mass.: Charlesbridge Publishing.**
This is a charming fictionalized story of a young boy, Jacques, who lives for a short time in the same Arles, France boarding house as the famous painter, Vincent van Gogh. Jacques learns from Vincent's life, and his ways of seeing and creating, as they share many wonderful moments and memories. The fanciful story is full of rich biographical detail about the life and works of the painter, as seen through the eyes of

a young person. The book's illustrations are in the expressive style of van Gogh from his Arles period.

Application: Use as a creative catalyst in informal, cross-grade performance sharing of the book in which older students read aloud to younger children. As they do so, students could show a "living gallery" of appropriate van Gogh prints or students' own paintings in the style of van Gogh (in displays or simply held above their heads).

Waldman, N. (1999). *The starry night.* **Honesdale, Pa.: Boyds Mills.**
This narrative account of a boy who meets Vincent van Gogh is fictionalized with rich dialogue. The two of them visit a museum and find some of van Gogh's paintings.

Application: Use to introduce "museum behavior" or as a writing prompt for students to create dialogues with an artist of their choice.

Claude Monet

Bjork, C. (1985) *Linnea in Monet's garden.* **New York: R & S Books.**
Within engaging narrative style, this is an excellent fictionalized story of a little girl and her friend's loving pilgrimage to Claude Monet's famous painting environment (home and gardens) in Giverny, France. Linnea is pictured within the actual photographed settings (and his paintings of these scenes) where Monet painted his greatest works.

Application: After reading this wonderful story, pair with the following books, which show many of Monet's paintings and engage readers in hands-discovery activities about his art works.

Books to Pair with Artist Study of Monet

Armstrong, C. (1995). *My Monet art museum.* **New York: Philomel.**
Applications: This text gives young readers important cues to help find and place artwork stickers (actual reproductions of twenty of Monet's famous paintings found on miniature peel-off stickers at the back of this book) in the appropriate location to match the narrative presentation of his works. An answer key is provided, if young art-loving readers are stumped!

Also, use ideas in the book to create classroom bulletin boards about Monet, journal writing responses to his works, group discussions about each piece of artwork, and creative dramatizations of Monet's life and works. Alternatively, ask students to develop games to identify Monet's paintings.

Boutan, M. (1995). *Monet: Art activity pack.* **New York: Chronicle Books.**
Developed in collaboration with Paris's Musee d'Orsay, museum of Impressionist art, this excellent child-centered instructional packet includes a beautiful color book about Monet, his paintings, and the art techniques used.

   Application: This engaging art activity book features interesting ideas for related class art projects. The activity packet includes blank pages for students to create their own art and journal entries. A large-format poster is also included for the coloring activity. Other books in this series by the same author and publisher feature the life and works of Cezanne, Degas, Gauguin, Matisse, Picasso, Renoir, Rousseau, and van Gogh.

Degas

Littlesugar, A. (1999*). Marie in fourth position: The story of Degas' "The Little Dancer."* **New York: Paperstar.**
This book explains the story and paintings of Degas's impressions of the Paris ballet dancers.

   Application: Use for interactive discussions of the books paintings and how artists capture specific events and actions. Compare and contrast several paintings of different artists who use thematic material (i.e., horses, the sea, houses and buildings, people, landscapes, seasons, and other themes) within their works.

Additional Artist Study

Ringgold, F., Feeman, L., & Roucher, N. (1996). *Talking to Faith Ringgold.* **New York: Crown.**
Internationally known African American artist Faith Ringgold has created many paintings, soft sculptures, masks, and story quilts, as well as children's books, such as *Tar Beach* (1991, Crown Publishers) and *Aunt Harriet's Underground Railroad in the Sky* (1995, Crown Publishers). In this revealing and sensitively written book, Ringgold talks about her childhood and developing artistry, all the while speaking directly to young readers through her narrative, as if they were conversing with

her in her home studio. She pairs her personal story with photos of her original works, works of art influencing her work, as well as current and historical photos and events in America, such as the evolution of jazz or the civil rights movement.

Application: Within her story, the author suggests journal writing activities and group discussion topics. She also includes suggestions for children's creative art experimentation and exploration paired with learning about elements of art: "How many different ways can you draw a tree, a bird, or any other object? Will you use thick lines or thin lines? Dark or light colors? Shading or outlining? Patterns and textures or flat colors? Think of all the possibilities and then draw your object several ways." Use questions from the author in group discussions before active art experimentation in your classroom.

Sellier, M. (1996). *Chagall from a to z.* **New York: Bedrick Books.**
Biographical and artwork information are presented in an A-to-Z format, in which each letter of the alphabet is paired with information about Chagall and examples of his paintings. Other artists featured in books by the same author and publisher are: *Matisse from A to Z* (1995) and *Bonnard from A to Z* (1997).

Application: This collection could be used to create bulletin boards or student-created books, such as "My Favorite Artists and Paintings."

Stanley, D. (2000). *Michelangelo.* **New York: HarperCollins.**
This book describes the artistic life of Michelangelo, including his sculpture and painting. Tracing his life and his artistic interest, the author uses a unique combination of photographs and illustrations to make her point.

Application: This book contains a great deal of information. You might want students to read different parts and then share their section of the book with peers in the class. The message for students is that artists can work in multiple media to share their ideas.

Winter, J. (1998). *My name is Georgia.* **San Diego: Harcourt Brace.**
This book focuses on the life of Georgia O'Keefe. The author suggests that, from the time she was very young, Ms. O'Keefe saw the world in her own way. The illustrations are filled with color and include replicas of the artist's work.

Application: This book could be used to introduce biographies (see Krull and the Venezia collection) or for an introduction to painting flowers in the O'Keefe style.

Krull, K. (1995). *Lives of the artists: Masterpieces, messes, and what the neighbors thought.* **San Diego: Harcourt Brace.**
This book introduces readers to eighteen artists by providing a glimpse into their lives. The author likes to add details that make each artist interesting, such as the fact that Matisse quit law school and his wife opened a hat shop.

Venezia, M. (1994-2001). *Getting to know the world's greatest artists.* **New York: Children's Press.**
This is a comprehensive series for children about the progression of art through the lives and works of famous painters. The engaging format includes informative, colorful cartooned captions, adding interest and contemporary spark for young readers' imaginations.

Applications: Use this book in biography/discovery group activities like "All About _____," in which students are asked to find out ten important facts about an individual artist's life, as well as to describe ten of the artist's paintings. Toward this end, the following painters are each featured within additional individual books in this series by Venezia: Frida Kahlo, Grant Wood, Andy Warhol, El Greco, Edward Hopper, Francisco Goya, Pieter Bruegel, Marc Chagall, Paul Klee, Henri De Toulouse-Lautrec, Paul Gaugian, Paul Cezanne, Henri Mattisse, Pierre Auguste Renoir, Monet, Picasso, Salvador Dali, Rockwell, Diego Rivera, Michelangelo, Dorothea Lange, Mary Cassatt, Grant Wood, Rembrandt, O'Keefe, van Gogh, Goya, Jackson Pollock, Alexander Calder, da Vinci, Raphael, Botticelli, and Degas.

Books about Drama and Dance

Allen, D. (2000). *Dancing in the wings.* **New York: Dial Books for Young Readers.**
This book introduces Sassy, a young girl who thinks that her feet are too big for her to ever become a ballerina. For now, she's just dancing in the wings, never in front of others.

Asher, S. (2001). *Stella's dancing days.* **San Diego: Harcourt Brace.**
A story of a dancing Stella, who just happens to be a kitten! Everyday events hold unlimited opportunities for Stella to stretch, sing, and dance through life.

Application: Use in read-alouds paired with improvised movements that the younger children will naturally and gladly create.

McMahon, P. (2000). *Dancing wheels.* **Boston: Houghton Mifflin.**
Meet the dancing group in which some of the dancers are "sit-down" and others are "stand-up" dancers. This book provides a behind-the-scene look at a dance troop that includes people with and without disabilities.

Walton, R., and Lopez-Escriva, A. (2001). *How can you dance?* **New York: GP Putnam's Sons.**
Written in clever poetic text, this book sends the message that dancing is very, very important. Each page provides a reason that you might not dance (e.g., how can you dance when one foot's sore?) and a solution to keep dancing (e.g., dance on the other foot).

Books about Music

Books with Song Texts

Children love to see, hear, and sing as they begin to read and understand song texts. These reading/singing activities can be encouraged by inviting children to do some of the following:

- Listen to recordings of songs as the book is shown (point to the song text) to students and begin to sing along (with students) to that text.
- Invite the children to answer some of the following kinds of questions: What is the song about? What happens in the song? How do we know? What are your favorite parts of the song? Why?
- Ask children to point to the words of the song as they read and listen, and sing again from that book. Write appropriate song texts on a large chart for group read-alouds.
- Invite small groups of students to create movement and dramatizations for song verses that can be performed for others in the class as the song is sung by all.
- Encourage the students to write out the text, write about the song, and illustrate favorite sections for class books and displays on bulletin boards about "songs we know in books we love."

The following books are suggested for creative song text response:

Birdseye, T., and Birdseye, G. (1994). *She'll be comin' round the mountain.* New York: Holiday House.
Catalano, D. (1998). *Frog went a-courting: A musical play in six acts.* Honesdale, Pa.: Boyds Mills Press.
Conrad, P. (1985). *Prairie songs.* New York: HarperCollins.

Manson, C. (1993). *Over the river and through the wood*. New York: North-South Books.

Mattox, C. (1989). *Shake it to the one that you live the best: Play songs and lullabies from black musical traditions*. Nashville, Tenn.: JTG.

McGill, A. (2000). *In the hallow of your hand: Slave lullabies*. Boston: Houghton Mifflin.

Milnes, G. (1990). *Granny will your dog bite and other mountain rhymes*. New York: Knopf.

Raschka, C. (1998). *Simple Gifts*. New York: Holt.

Saport, L. (1999). *All the pretty little horses: A traditional lullaby*. New York: Clarion Books.

Spier, P. (1970). *The Erie Canal*. New York: Doubleday.

Taback, S. (1999). *Joseph had a little overcoat*. New York: Viking.

Weiss, G., and Thiele, B. (1967). *What a wonderful world*. Littleton, Mass.: Sundance.

Westcott, N. (1989). *Skip to my lou*. Boston: Little & Brown.

Winter, J. (1998). *Follow the drinking gourd*. New York: Knopf.

Yolen, J. (1992). *Street rhymes around the world*. Honesdale, Pa.: Boyds Mills Press.

POETRY AND RHYTHMIC TEXT (MUSIC AND MOVEMENT)

Applications: Invite students to read aloud or silently read poetry and/or rhythmic text about music and music making. Discuss meanings of that text. If students are participating in a group read-aloud, ask them how they think the words should be spoken: soft or loud, fast or slow, punctuated or emphasized, etc. If text is placed on an overhead or large chart, mark the students' ideas for expressive speech with colored marks above appropriate sections of the text. Design the symbol markings together, as a class. Lead read-alouds by pointing to the text as the children read together expressively.

Whenever possible, play CDs or cassettes in the style of the music featured in the text during expressive, poetic speech. For instance, if the poem or text is about jazz, play a jazz recording to use as background music and allow for silences before or within the read-aloud so that the music can be featured. The following books contain poetry and rhythmic text for creative reader response:

Hopkins, L. (1997). *Song and dance*. New York: Simon and Schuster.
A collection of wonderful poetry about dance, jazz, sounds of the city

streets, rap, and more. Great for children's creative movement ideas as poems are read aloud.

Igus, T. (1998). *I see the rhythm.* **San Francisco: Children's Book Press.**
The author and illustrator created this superb rhythmic text about the development of jazz—from pre-jazz influences of Western Africa to today's popular forms of music. The book's colorful and dramatically lettered text is vibrantly linked to illustrations and historical developments surrounding periods of jazz history, including swing, bebop, cool, etc. Many jazz artists are mentioned; share samples from these artists with students.

Jabar, C. (1992). *Shimmy shake earthquake: Don't forget to dance poems.* **Boston: Little, Brown.**
Students will enjoy creating movement and other artistic responses to the fine poems in this collection.

Shields, C., and Junakovic, S. (2000). *Music.* **New York: Handprint Books.**
Mysterious animals, insects, and their instrument-playing action are described in this engaging text and then shown within fold-out illustrations of the creatures and the instruments they play. For example, "I'm a big fellow. I love to play cello. The sound that it makes is so sweet and mellow. I can play music most anywhere. For I am . . . (readers then open the folded page) . . . a cello who's also a **bear**." This book is great for learning about instruments, exploratory movement and dramatization, and developing new vocabulary about music making.

LEARNING TO LISTEN TO MUSIC

Texts describing how people listen to music, as well as those highlighting the corresponding musical sound characteristics of various kinds of instruments, have always been popular with music lovers of all ages! As an added bonus, teachers and parents alike can learn more about music as they read and listen together. You might suggest these books and book/CD pairings for school library resources, musical listening resources within your classroom, or within additional reading lists or educational gift suggestions for parents and grandparents/guardians to consider.

The following books provide excellent learning opportunities for imaginative discussions, musical listening activities, and other creative reader response:

Deetlefs, R. (1999). *The song of six birds*. **New York: Dutton Children's Books.**
This charmingly illustrated story focuses on a West African girl who is given a wooden flute, but cannot make music until she learns to beautifully imitate musical sounds from wonderful animals that she meets in the forest.

Application: Use in a read-aloud for word play, for instrument pantomimes using creative movement, as writing prompts, and for other student-designed creative movement about this story.

Ganeri, A. (1996). *The young person's guide to the orchestra: Benjamin Britten's composition on CD narrated by Ben Kingsley*. **San Diego: Harcourt Brace.**
This book and CD are an enthralling children's classic to be equally enjoyed by young people and adults of all ages. Many musical listening segments, photos, and illustrations of the instruments are included.

Application: This book might be used in sections over several days. Teachers might want to invite older students to play various instruments for younger students. Alternatively, this book could be paired with a showing of Disney's *Fantasia* and other videos about the orchestra and orchestral music.

Gollub, M. (2000). *The jazz fly*. **Santa Rosa, Calif.: Tortuga Press.**
Learn about jazz (scat) through this very "hip," humorous, and informative story and fantastic CD about a little fly who goes on to jam with the pros!

Application: Encourage the students to point to this engaging text as they follow along and listen, learning the sound, feel, and look of jazz, jazz players, instruments, and improvisation.

Levine, R. (2000). *Story of the orchestra: A child's introduction to the instruments, the music, the musicians and composers*. **New York: Black Dog & Leventhal.**
This book focuses on the orchestra and all its components.

Application: It would be useful to suggest this book to students who have questions about orchestras before seeing an orchestra play or during class discussions about large groups of musicians working together.

Kuskin, K. (1982). *The philharmonic gets dressed.* **New York: HarperCollins.**
An introduction to what musicians do and how they make music together through a day in the life of a musician.
Application: A great classroom activity would be to invite community musicians to come and perform their music, share informally about their instrument and their lives as music makers.

Shaik, F. (1998). *The jazz of our street.* **New York: Dial.**
This beautifully illustrated, evocative story set in New Orleans centers around a group of children who wait anxiously for the local jazz street band to play their beloved music throughout the neighborhood. Everyone joins in as the music sweeps the children and adults into richly expressive scenes of their enjoyment and participation in music and dance.
Application: Ask the students when and where they have seen and heard music making in their community. Ask them to illustrate and write about this occasion. What did the music sound like? What were people doing? How did the music make you feel?

Weatherford, C. (2000). *The sound that jazz makes.* **New York: Walter and Company**.
Students will enjoy learning all about jazz through this lyrical, rhythmic text (e.g., "JAZZ is a downbeat born in our nation, chords of struggle and jubilation, bursting forth from hearts set free in notes that echo history. This is the sound that jazz makes!) and realistic illustrations of music makers featured within the text.
Application: Use within informal performances for other classes in which students introduce the music of certain jazz greats by expressively reading aloud text about each artist before excerpts of that music are heard. Recorded music for this project can be found at local record stores in the Classic Jazz section under the name of the artist, or within library record collections or school district musical collections and basal text series in music.

Lives and Works of Composers

Applications: Invite children to read books about famous composers to create dramatizations about their lives and works through group or class projects, journal entries in student books about composers and their works, class bulletin boards, and for use within a quiet "learn about music" section of your classroom. Pair these books with relevant recordings (that come with the books or are found in local music stores).

Celenza, A. (2000). *The farewell symphony*. Watertown, Mass.: Charlesbridge Publishing.
This is the story and CD of Haydn's Symphony No. 45 ("Farewell").

Downing, J. (1994). *Mozart tonight*. New York: Alladin.
This text explains all about Mozart's life at the time of his compostion of the great opera *Don Giovanni*.

Fisher, L. (1996). *William Tell*. New York: Farrar, Straus, and Giroux.
This book invites readers to find out about the true story of the person featured in the *William Tell Overture* by the famous composer Rossini. Students will recognize this music because it is used in many children's cartoons.

Gatti, A. (1997). *The magic flute*. San Francisco, Calif.: Chronicle Books.
This book is a superbly illustrated retelling (with CD) of Wolfgang Mozart's whimsical, much-loved, fairy-tale opera.
   Application: This book would be a great choice to read and discuss with older children and later encourage them to illustrate sections of the opera as they listen to the recording.

Isadora, R. (1994). *Firebird*. New York: Putnam.
   Application: This book could be paired with listening to a recording of "Firebird" ballet music by Igor Stravinsky. Unfortunately, the recording is not provided with the book.

Krull, K. (1993). *Lives of the musicians: Good times, bad times (and what the neighbors thought)*. San Diego: Harcourt Brace.
Excellent for older children interested in accurate, often humorous and poignant short biographies of nineteen famous composers. Included are

the European masters (Mozart, Bach, et al.), American popular composers (Stephen Foster, Scott Joplin, Gilbert and Sullivan, George Gershwin, and Woody Guthrie), and a few female composers (Clara Schumann and Nadia Boulanger).

Application: Use in bulletin board displays and student books/journals about "Our Favorite Composers."

Pinkney, A. D. (1998). *Duke Ellington: The piano prince and his orchestra.* **New York: Hyperion Books.**
This book focuses on the life, music, and times of this famous jazz composer, conductor, and performing artist.

Application: Compare the life of Duke Ellington to another composer/performer from an earlier era and location. What were some challenges Ellington had to face to become an artist and have his music be heard? Why? Use the Krull book for ideas.

Press, D. (1994). *A multicultural portrait of America's music.* **New York: Marshall Cavendish.**
This book would be especially useful for use within social studies contexts for older children interested in the history of American jazz and popular music.

Application: This is an excellent resource for student projects, displays, and reports about the history of jazz, rock, country, and folk music styles.

Price, L. (1990). *Aida.* **San Diego: Harcourt Brace.**
Beautifully illustrated retelling of Pucinni's famous opera plot (set in ancient Egypt) about the perils of an Ethiopian princess, Aida.

Application: Pair student read-alouds of this text with actual recorded music of the opera, *Aida.* Use sections of the text (matched to the order of the musical plot) to introduce short listening samples of that character's singing, choruses, duets, etc.

Vernon, R. (1997). *Introducing Stravinsky.* **Parsippany, N.J.: Silver Burdett Press.**
Richly detailed and visually pleasing biography of the life, work, and times of the great twentieth-century composer, Igor Stavinsky.

Application: Use information within this book within class discussions of Stravinsky's life and recorded music to the ballet *Firebird* within the book (same title). Add information to a class bulletin board of the lives and works of famous composers.

Vigna, G. (1999). *Masters of music: Jazz and its history.* **New York: Barron's.**
This is an excellent chronological book about jazz and its music makers.

   Application: Use to inform students during projects about jazz music and musicians.

Books About Instruments, Singers, and Music Making

Applications: Explore the following books to create your own classroom ideas for group and individual creative reader response through ideas for student group projects, book club discussions, student-created books about the literature, rewrites of the story paired with student illustrations, creative dramatizations of the book, pairings with listening to music appropriate to the text, and other ideas from discussions and collaborations with students and teaching colleagues:

Ardley, N. (2000). *Eyewitness books: Music: Discover the world of musical sound and the amazing variety of instruments that create music.* **New York: Dorling Kindersley.**
From ancient instruments of many cultures to modern computerized instruments and music making, this incredible sourcebook features thousands of photos and interesting facts about music and the science of musical sound.

Burleigh, R. (2001). *Lookin' for bird in the big city.* **New York: Harcourt Brace.**
This is a wonderful story of the young jazz trumpeter Miles Davis and his Harlem encounter with his musical idol, the great "Bird" saxophonist Charlie Parker.

Clement, C. (1989). *The voice of the wood.* **New York: Dial.**
An instrument maker lovingly crafts a cello out of a beloved tree.

Curtis, G. (1998). *The bat boy & his violin.* **New York: Simon and Schuster.**
Set in the South prior to racial integration, this is the story of a bat boy in the Negro baseball league. Although he loves baseball, Reginald worries that he won't be ready for his violin recital, so he practices in the dugout as the players grow to love his music.

Cutler, J. (1999). *The cello of Mr. O.* **New York: Dutton.**
The poignant and hopeful story of a musician who plays his cello in spite of the chaos and confusion of his war-torn World War II-era European city. A little girl is mesmerized and soothed by Mr. O's courageous playing in the middle of a turbulent war-torn street.

Dengler, M. (1999). *Fiddlin' Sam.* **Flagstaff, Ariz.: Rising Moon.**
Set in the Ozarks Mountains, an old fiddler named Sam went from town to town, sharing his music. As he became an old man, he searched for someone to carry his musical gifts to others.

Grifalconi, A. (1999). *Tiny's hat.* **New York: HarperCollins.**
This very tender story is based on the childhood of the great blues singer, Bessy Smith.

Hopkinson, D. (1999). *A band of angels: A story inspired by the jubilee singers.* **New York: Antheneum.**
This is the true story of the founding of the Fiske University Jubilee Singers in Nashville, Tennessee.

Isadora, R. (1979). *Ben's trumpet.* **New York: Greenwillow.**
This story for younger children is loosely based on the life of Louis Armstrong.

Johnson, A. (1996). *Picker McClickker.* **Nashville, Tenn.: Premium Press.**
Imagine the boy with the fastest hands. Soon, his amazing and humorous talents are applied to picking a country guitar.

Lacapa, M. (1990). *The flute player: An Apache folktale.* **Flagstaff, Ariz.: Northland Publishing.**
This is a lovely, authentic folktale of a Native American flute player and the girl who loves him. Written and illustrated by the well-known Hopi/Apache author, storyteller, and illustrator, Michael Lacapa.

London, J. (1993). *Hip cat.* **San Francisco: Chronicle Books.**
This book chronicles the adventures of a cool cat and his jazz music making.

McKee, D. (1991). *The sad story of Veronica who played the violin.* **New York: Kane, Miller.**
Meet Veronica, who plays the violin with exceptional skill. She is so good that she brings people to tears. One day, on a trip in the jungle, she is eaten by a lion. This is why people no longer dance in the street.

McPhail, D. (1999). *Mole music.* **New York: Henry Holt.**
This is a touching story about a little mole who learns to play the violin and imagines that his playing can save the world. Not venturing outside his underground home, the mole plays and plays while people above ground enjoy the music he makes.

Meyrich, C. (1989). *The musical life of Gustav Mole.* **New York: Child's Play International.**
Meyrich's book and cassette traces the life of Gustav, a mole, from babyhood to old age. Covers many genres of music and a variety of musical instruments, using solo, duets, trios, quartets, quintets, and a variety of instruments. After a long musical life, Gustav realizes his goal and becomes an accomplished composer.

Moss, L. (1995). *Zin! Zin! Zin! A violin.* **New York: Simon and Schuster.**
This book, with its high-energy artwork and engaging cumulative-type story, helps young readers learn about making music, instruments, and groupings of instruments.

Rockwell, N. (1967, 1994). *Willie was different: A children's story by Norman Rockwell.* **New York: Dragonfly Books.**
Rockwell's classic illustrated version about a little bird, Willie, who had the amazing talent of chirping back very complex musical selections he hears at the window of the practicing, flute-playing town librarian.

Schroeder, A. (1996). *Satchmo's blues.* **New York: Doubleday.**
This is a tender and lovingly illustrated account of the childhood of the great Louis "Satchmo" Armstrong.

Turner, B. (1996). *The living violin.* **New York: Knopf.**
This text focuses on the violin, its history, construction, and music through a wonderful CD pairing, illustrations, detailed photographs, and

interesting facts. Also included are sections about string instruments from other cultures, helping young readers gain perspective about the history and evolution of this popular Western string instrument.

CREATIVE MOVEMENT AND DANCE AND DRAMATIC RESPONSE TO LITERATURE

A child's response to literature can naturally evolve into active, emotive, and expressive performances of creative movement (dance) and drama (theatre) (McCaslin, 1990). In this way, the arts of dance and theatre can be integrated when viewed as combined, expressive vehicles or creative mediums for active reader responses to literature. Hancock (2000) describes these types or modes of response to literature as including elements of creative and dramatic movement, choral readings, readers' theatre, and puppetry and plays. Concerning the nature of these reader responses, Hancock adds:

> Children's literature must be read, listened to, and savored before any form of dramatic response can result. A child must feel a familiarity with the text, establish a kinship with characters, internalize the plot sequence, and develop a joy in the language and style before they can be expected to respond expressively. The lived through experience of repeated readings of the text prepares the performer for the task at hand. Literature of all genres inspires dramatic response but requires immersion, freedom to be oneself, and a growing sense of confidence before the dramatic response is shared. . . . for younger children, dramatic response is spontaneous and unencumbered. . . . Older children prefer some time for informal rehearsal for collaborative efforts, but expression, not perfection, is always the priority of dramatic response. (p. 254)

The following is a list of children's books and teaching applications designed to actively engage students in creative responses involving dance (creative movement) and theatre:

McKissack, P. (1997). *Mirandy and brother wind.* **New York: Dragonfly.**
Set within the forty years immediately following slavery, this book is the story of Mirandy and her dream to enter and win the local cakewalk dance contest. The cakewalk is a nineteenth-century popular dance with roots in African American culture. The dance features high-stepping

couples strutting in very regal, grand-march fashion (Levene, 1993). In this story, Mirandy knows she could be a success if only she could dance with her favorite companion, the wind! This beautifully illustrated, Coretta Scott King award-winning book is beautifully written and speaks to young children's imaginations and to the desire to move and pretend.

Application: Pair the reading of this book with prompts from the text for student creative movement. Retell this story as a performance with "spaces" for the children to act out and creatively move as how they imagine Mirandy might move within the action of the story. Pair students' creative movements with appropriate recorded music, "Golliwog's Cakewalk" by Claude Debussy, and the ragtime music of Scott Joplin. A poem that can be easily connected to *Mirandy and Brother Wind* is "Who Has Seen the Wind?," a poem by Christina Rosetti within *Windy Day: Stories and Poems* (Bauer, 1988). The poem paints a picture in the young reader's mind about how the wind can be seen in the objects and things it touches and moves.

Schroeder, A. (1989). *Ragtime Tumpie*. Boston: Little & Brown.
This is a fictionalized account of the young childhood of the world-famous ragtime dancer, Josephine Baker (known as "Tumpie" in her early years). Tumpie was inspired by the beautiful music of Scott Joplin and simply could not stop dancing to the music she loved so much.

Application: Allow the students to hear the music Tumpie loved by playing recordings of Joplin Rags ("The Entertainer," "Maple Leaf Rag," and others). Consult your state music series text to locate selections of appropriate ragtime piano music by Scott Joplin. Allow the children to clap on and off the beats and explore moving in syncopated ways to the engaging rhythms of these pieces. How did Tumpie move? Create a class movement to use in read-aloud performances of this book for other classes. Discuss the places and settings discussed in this book, as well as the musical terms and instruments mentioned.

Martin, B. and Archambault, J. (1986). *Barn dance*. New York: Henry Holt.
A little boy is awakened by strange festivities and music coming from the barn. The farm animals are all involved in a night time, rhythmic hoe down, complete with their unusual sounds and square dancing.

Application: This rhythmic text is ideal for expressive read-alouds and as an introduction to square dancing. Invite a local square dance instructor or caller to your classroom to teach a beginning dance to the children. Appropriate music to pair with read-alouds of this book include such pieces as "Rodeo" by the American composer Aaron Copland, "Old Joe Clark" traditional fiddle tune and song, and the traditional American songs, "Cumberland Gap," "Buffalo Gals," and "Turkey in the Straw."

Pinkney, A. (1993). *Alvin Ailey.* **New York: Hyperion.**
The great New York choreographer began his interest in dance through his gospel music experiences during his childhood in Texas, later in his youth in Los Angeles, and finally in his residency in New York. For older children, this book is the story of Ailey's developing artistry, choreography, and the founding of his famous New York modern dance company.

Application: Pair the study of this book with class viewings of videos of Alvin Ailey's famous dance piece, "Revelations." Videocassettes of this piece can be located through Amazon.com and other on-line video distributors. Discuss with the students how this dance piece could have been influenced by Ailey's childhood experiences with gospel music.

Glassman, B. (2001). *Mikail Baryshnikov: Dance genius.* **New York: Blackbirch.**
The life and work of Baryshnikov are presented within this book for older children. The book features interviews with the famous dancer and choreographer.

Applications: Pair the study of this famous ballet dancer with video of his performances. Analyze the styles of dance you see on video. Is Baryshnikov exclusively a classical ballet dancer or has he experimented with other dance styles (jazz, modern)? What choreographers has he worked under? (George Balanchine and Twyla Tharp). What are some of his famous works? What is he doing in his career right now? Create a scrapbook of his life and works, as well as the life and works of other famous dances of many genres: ballet, modern, hip hop, multicultural, etc.

Cooper, E. (2001) *Dance.* **New York: Greenwillow.**
We catch a glimpse of the real lives of dancers and choreographers (as well as stage directors and staff, costumers, makeup artists, and lighting technicians) from rehearsal to opening night. This book is the tale of how dancers train, rehearse, and finally perform after months of disciplined hard work.

Application: Invite professional dancers to talk to your class before staged performances at your school or community venue. Ask community professionals if interested students could view dress rehearsals and preparations backstage. Invite students to interview dance performers about their lives, work, and performance. Create a class "newpaper" article about a performance of dance, including a critique of that performance.

Glover, S., Weber, B., and Hines, G. (2000). *Savion—My life in tap*. New York: Morrow.
The story of Savion Glover, the famous tap dancer, as told by the artist and author/dancer collaborators on this book, Gregory Hines and Bruce Weber.

Application: Pair the study of this book with viewing a video of tap performances by Gregory Hines and others (available through Amazon.com). Ask students who study tap to demonstrate for the class. Invite community tap artists to your school. View video of popular performing artist, such as Stomp, Riverdance, and others.

BOOKS FOR DRAMATIC RESPONSE

Poetry adapted to choral readings is one of many simple and effective ways to elicit children's dramatic responses (see chapter 4). Other substantial avenues for dramatic expression already articulated within this book can be found when children read aloud actual words and speeches of famous historical figures (see chapter 5), script and perform retellings, or actual scenes from children's literature (see chapter 7), and create original movement and drama performances of legends and tales from many cultural origins (see chapter 5). Within these varied expressive and dramatic activities, children are able to orally share their reading experiences through using expressive speech, dialogue, dynamics, rhythm, tempo, movement, characterization, plot, and other integrated components of music, dance, visual arts, and theatre. In addition, in order to create these dramatic expressions, children are reading and rereading, learning new vocabulary, and actively experimenting with learning based on and framed by standards and content found in the arts, as well as content and standards within other subject areas (see chapter 1).

We have offered many children's literature sources and teaching applications designed to actively engage students in reading through the arts. What follows is a direct model of a teaching unit designed to introduce upper elementary and middle school students to string music, instruments, and musicians through activity tied to children's literature.

A SAMPLE INTEGRATED ARTS UNIT: STRINGS ATTACHED

The challenge of fully engaging young students in meaningful musical listening experiences can be a lifelong career goal for many of us. Varied listening experiences involving instrument identification, characteristic sound, timbre, instrument groupings, as well as various historical contexts involving multiple musical styles and genres are key components within a comprehensive education in music (MENC, 1994). Ideas for planning, creating, teaching, and assessing introductory listening lessons about Western string instruments are, therefore, a part of the overall "big picture" concerning general music instruction. A music teacher's ability to easily access and actively experiment with creative, usable resources can serve to build or augment their existing teaching repertoire of successful listening experiences, including those introducing Western string instruments. Additionally, in many elementary and middle school settings, teachers are seeking appropriate instructional links to the general curriculum, which could serve to heighten student interest and involvement through connecting music to other school learning activities.

With these instructional needs in mind, this section offers an example of an introductory curriculum unit pairing musical listening activities with children's literature about string instruments. There are several reasons to connect musical listening activities with children's literature. First, the purposeful and creative connection of music with language arts and social studies can create engaging lesson entry-points designed to capture the child's interest with involvement in the music of Western string instruments (e.g., Jacobs, 1989; McDonald and Fisher, 1999a). Second, beyond engaging students, integrated curriculum provides students with a depth of knowledge about a topic of study and makes the connections between the disciplines more explicit (Jacobs, 1997). Similarily, according to the National Standards in Music:

> Effective learning is not subject to the artificial boundaries traditionally separating subject matter in school. Ultimately the outcomes of schooling must cut across subject-matter fields in order to be useful. Each of the arts must maintain its integrity in the curriculum and be taught for its own sake, but at the same time the curriculum should emphasize relationships among the arts and relationships between the arts and disciplines outside the arts. (MENC, 1994b, p. 4)

Through purposeful instructional pairing of quality children's literature and music, students can become immersed in contexts and personal meanings of the story's and poem's direct links to musical sound and vice versa (e.g., McDonald, 2000b). Specific literature and poetry selections have been carefully chosen because of their potential to create thematic environments for imaginative musical listening to string instruments. Our criteria for choosing quality poetry and children's literature for this integrated listening unit included:

- direct, believable, and accurate references to types of music, musicians, music-making, or musical instruments within a book's story line or poetic text.
- texts that create enough "space" or curiosity on the part of the reader (i.e., "I wonder what that music sounds like?") to enable the teacher to layer musical listening experiences within the story without changing the mood and context of the child's reading or read-to experience.
- an accurate portrayal of historical periods or cultural settings coupled with engaging art and excellent illustrations that enhance visual learning.
- sources that accurately reflect the multicultural nature of today's diverse school populations.

Student activities within this model curriculum unit include:

- created movement and drama performances to stories and recorded string music (National Standards 6, 7, 8).
- musical listening within story settings (children's literature contexts) (National Standards 6, 7, 8).
- identification of Western string instruments by sound and sight (National Standard 6).
- listening to, analyzing, responding to, and reflecting upon various types of string music, such as solo, chamber, Western orchestral, bluegrass, and contemporary (National Standards 6, 7, 9).
- awareness of eras of history and culture, including twentieth-century American and European historical references (Westward expansion, the Great Depression, World War II, civil rights, and cultural diversity) through visual art, photography, and biography of the people of the times (National Standards 8 and 9).
- directed writing experiences including student poetry, journals, and illustrated class books based on musical listening and related children's literature (National Standards 6, 7, 8, 9).

In addition to these classroom activities, we provide classroom-management suggestions and strategies to improve classroom musical listening environments, suggestions for further listening, children's literature links to string and orchestral music, and suggestions for teaching collaborations and curriculum planning.

A MODEL INTRODUCTORY LISTENING UNIT

This listening unit is organized into three episodes. All of these episodes are stages of the unit and will require between one and three class sessions, depending on the amount of time a teacher chooses to focus on strings. These episodes include suggestions for extended student learning through partnerships with classroom teachers who may be interested in the small group, cooperative learning processes and performances of the music book club selections described in the following section. Thus, this unit allows music classroom activities to become a focus within language arts instruction. Sources include materials appropriate for grades three through six.

Episode #1

To introduce this unit, bring one or more string instruments to class and show pictures of a wide variety of string instruments to students. For background music, use one of the listening selections from table 6.1. Engage students in a preliminary class discussion using some of the following questions and list student responses on the board: Have

Table 6.1.   Musical Listening Selections

Violin
Brahams "1st Movement" Sonata for Violin and Piano in G Major and "1st Movement" Violin concerto in A Major, K. 219
Paganini "24 Caprices"
Rimsky-Korsakov "Capriccio espagnol"
Tchaikovsky "Symphony No. 4 in F minor, Op. 36" (3rd movement: pizzicato ostinato throughout)

Viola
Berlioz "Harold in Italy," Op. 16, 1st Movement: Harold's Theme
Brahams "Geistliches Wiegenlied," Op. 91, No. 2 (Joseph, lieber Joseph mein)
Ippolitov-Ivanov "In the Village"
Kodaly "Third Movement" (Song), Hary Janos Suite and "Serenade for Two Violins and Viola"
Stravinsky "The Rite of Spring" (Mysterious Circle of the Adolescents)

Table 6.1. Musical Listening Selections (continued)

Cello
Haydn "Divertimento for Cello and Orchestra"
Kodaly "Duo for Violin and Cello" and "Sonata for Solo Cello"
Penderecki "Sonata for Cello and Orchestra"
Rossini "At Dawn," William Tell Overture
Schubert "Symphony No. 8 in B minor (Unfinished)" principal theme
Schumann "Concerto in A minor for Cello and Orchestra," Op. 129

Double Bass
Beethoven "Symphony No. 5 in C minor," Op. 67, (third movement)
Mahler 3rd Movement of "Symphony No. 1"
Saint-Saens "Elephant, V. from Carnival of the Animals"

Assorted String Chamber and Orchestral Music
Bach, J.S. "Double Violin Concerto in e minor"
Barber "Adagio for Strings"
Berg "String Quartet," Op. 3
Copland "Rodeo (Hoe Down)" and "Appalachian Spring" (Shaker Tune-Simple Gifts
    section opening)
Corelli "Suite for Strings" (Gigue and Sarabande)
Debussy "En Bateau (In a Boat)"
Kodaly "String Quartets"
Mendelssohn "Concerto in e Minor for Violin and Orchestra" (third movement)
Penderecki "String Quartet"
Rimsky-Korsakov Scheherazade, Op. 35, Movement 1 "The Sea and Sinbad's Ship"
Rossini-Respighi "Pizzicato" (Fantastic Toyshop)
Tchaikovsky "Serenade in C Major for Strings," Op. 48
Vaughn-Williams "Lark Ascending"
Vivaldi "The Four Seasons—Spring"

Bluegrass/Appalachian Fiddle Music: CD recordings
High Lonesome: The Story of Bluegrass Music—Original Motion Picture Soundtrack.
    (1993). CMH.
Appalachian Stomp: Bluegrass Classics by Bill Monroe et al. (1995).
    Wea/Atlantic/Rhino.
Bluegrass Breakdown: 14 Instrumentals (1998). Uni/Easydisc.

Hybrid Styles, Bluegrass and Chamber Music: CD recordings
Appalachian Waltz (1996). Sony Classics # 68460
Appalachian Journey (2000). Sony Classics # 66782

Early Music featuring Strings (viola da gamba)
CD recordings by the group Hespèrion XX (Jordi Savall's Group):
Music from Christian and Jewish Spain (1999). Emd/Virgin Classics.
Hespèrion XX—Middle Ages & Renaissance (1997). Fontalis.
Elizabethan Consort Music 1558–1603 (1998). Alia Vox.
Dowland: Lachrimae or Seaven Teares (1994). Fontalis.

you seen different string instruments? Where? What kind of music were they playing? What kinds of musical groups use string instruments? Following this introductory conversation, hold up one of the string instruments. Invite students into a more-focused discussion with the following questions: How do strings make sounds? Where do the strings connect to the instrument? How are they adjusted? Are the strings different lengths? Do long strings make different sounds than short strings? Demonstrate the answers offered by students on the instruments. Allow each student to touch one of the instruments. Show instrument posters of violin, viola, cello, and double bass as you discuss these four instruments, allowing the students to hear a short recorded sample of each instrument.

Create a customized activity in which pictures, instrument posters, or overheads are used as the students listen to different samples of string instrument music. For example, you might have six short listening samples (thirty to sixty seconds) of single instruments or ensembles, as well as six corresponding pictures of people playing instruments labeled with the name of the instruments involved. Each of the six visuals can be matched with one of the recorded listening samples.

Many teachers admit to discipline and management problems during initial listening activities (McDonald, 2000). Before students listen to the samples, it might be helpful to structure the experience behaviorally by holding up your index finger. Ask the students to do the same. Tell the students that this "#1" means that everyone freezes and listens silently. Next, tell the students when they see two fingers up, they get to silently try to identify which picture matches the sound they are hearing, keeping those answers to themselves. When they see three fingers up, they then write the name of the instrument they think is playing for that selection on an answer sheet (i.e., #1 = violin). After they write down the name of the instrument, students should be encouraged to pantomime playing the instrument (behavior allowing) until the teacher displays his or her index finger again, indicating that a new instrument recording is playing. This nonverbal focusing activity establishes positive musical listening behaviors and allows both teacher and students to listen to the music without verbal interruptions.

After students have listened to each of the selections and recorded their answers, the teacher then reviews and replays each example, asking the students to check their answers and write in the correct answers, where needed. During this initial listening activity, significant vocabu-

Table 6.2.   Let's Find Out About Strings (Vocabulary Chart)

Word	What I Think It Means	What It Really Means	Where I Found Out
strings			
bow			
tuning			
pegs			
fingerboard			
bridge			
sound hole			
plucked			
string family			
violin			
viola			
cello			
double bass			
fiddle			
string section			
orchestra			
rehearsal			
performance			

lary will have been introduced. Take time now to encourage students to complete the prediction column in table 6.2.

As students participate in this unit, they should be encouraged to complete the remaining columns in their "Let's Find Out about Strings" vocabulary chart. For example, if the term *rehearsal* is used in class, students may check their understanding of the word and either confirm their knowledge or write a new entry. This activity establishes an understanding of the words necessary to communicate about musical listening.

Episode #2

Table 6.3 provides a list of videos appropriate for this musical-listening lesson on string instruments. Themes identified in these videos include the need for practice to master an instrument, the role

Table 6.3.   Video Sources About Strings and String Musicians

Instrument	Video	Description
Violin	*Fiddler on the Roof.* MGM/UA Studios (1971)	The film of this famous musical includes an opening segment played by a fiddler whose music is played by Isaac Stern.
Violin	*In the Fiddler's House.* Sony Classics (1995)	Interesting and entertaining biography and excellent musical performances of Itzhak Perlman, the famous Israeli American.
Violin	*Music of the Heart*, Walt Disney Home Video (1999)	This popular film portrays the real life story of an inner city string music teacher and her triumphant concert at Carnegie hall.
Cello	*Inspired by Bach No. 1–6.* Sony Classics (1996)	Famous cellist Yo Yo Ma plays six cello suites by Bach within six separate videos set in interesting environments—gardens, woods, homes, etc.
Assorted	*Fantasia.* Walt Disney Home Video (1939)	Stunning visual fantasies set to assorted classical music.
Assorted	*Fantasia 2000.* Disney Studios (1999)	Stunning visual fantasies set to assorted classical music.
Assorted	*From Mao to Mozart: Isaac Stern in China* [Excerpts]. Silver Burdett Ginn Music Magic Video Library (1991)	This video combines western classical music with traditional Chinese instruments.
Assorted	*String instruments: Bowed.* Silver Burdett Ginn Music Magic Video Library (1991)	Episodes on this video include performances on the violin by a young violinist at age 3, 9, 12, and adult showing her development on the instrument. This video also includes quality, short solo and group professional performances of all the string instruments.

of music in everyday life, the work of a musician, connecting visual and auditory experiences, and the kinds of music string instruments can play in various contexts. However, as most of us know, simply playing a video does not guarantee student learning and more often invites student misbehavior. Learning from video experiences is heightened if students are reminded that they are looking for information to complete the "Let's Find Out About Strings" journal assignment. Learning from videos is also enhanced when students know that they are expected to write about and discuss events from the videos.

For instance, an appropriate writing extension for videos about young string players could center around the question "describe what you think a young person has to do to learn to play a string instrument well." Alternatively, invite students to predict how Itzhak Perlman would respond to questions about his disability, his love for music, and his ability to play. Ask students to create both the questions and the answers they think Perlman might give to answer these questions by writing out this interview in their journals. A class discussion might focus on the connections between visual and auditory experiences after students viewed clips of either or both versions of *Fantasia*. Clearly, students are using vocabulary and musical concepts gained through these introductory lessons as they discuss and write about their musical listening experiences.

Episode #3

By this point in this unit, the students should have a considerable knowledge of string instruments, string music, musicians, and the contexts in which this music is played. They have learned this information through visuals, audio, dialogue, and journal-writing activities. Students are now ready to explore children's literature in which string music themes occur. Many of these books offer the added bonus of presenting cultural and historical contexts of string music-making. We believe that episodes 1 and 2 have prepared students for a level of understanding and interaction with the meanings, metaphors, and story lines presented in the upcoming children's book selections. We submit that many students would have a limited understanding of these texts without the prior knowledge gained through these direct listening experiences with string music and instruments.

Book clubs provide students an opportunity to read and discuss literature in small groups. Most often, students work in groups of four to six. All members of each group read the same book (see table 6.4 for suggested selections). Thus, in a class of twenty-six students, a teacher could select five or six different books and assign them to evenly divided small groups. Each group sits in a circle. If enough

Table 6.4.   Sources of Children's Literature: Annotated

Curtis, G. (1998). *The bat boy & his violin*. New York: Simon and Schuster.
Set in the south prior to integration, this is the story of a boy who is the bat boy in the
  Negro baseball league. Although he loves baseball, Reginald worries that he won't
  be ready for his violin recital and practices in the dugout as the players grow to love
  his music.

Cutler, J. (1999). *The cello of Mr. O*. New York: Dutton.
The poignant and hopeful story of a musician who plays his cello in spite of the chaos
  and confusion of his war-torn WWII European city environment. A little girl is
  mesmerized and soothed by Mr. O's courageous playing in the middle of a turbulent
  war-torn street scene.

Dengler, M. (1999). *Fiddlin' Sam*. Flagstaff, Ariz.: Rising Moon.
Set in the Ozarks Mountains, an old fiddler named Sam went from town to town
  sharing his music. As he became an old man, he searched for someone to learn to
  carry on his musical gifts to others.

Johnson, A. (1996). *Picker McClickker*. Nashville, Tenn.: Premium Press.
Imagine the boy with the fastest hands. Soon his amazing talents are applied to picking
  a country guitar.

McKee, D. (1991). *The sad story of Veronica who played the violin*. New York: Kane,
  Miller.
Meet Veronica who plays the violin with exceptional skill. She is so good that she brings
  people to tears. One day, on a trip in the jungle, she is eaten by a lion which explains
  why people no longer dance in the street.

McPhail, D. (1999). *Mole music*. New York: Henry Holt.
Meet the mole who learns to play the violin and imagines that his playing can save the
  world. While not venturing outside his underground home, the mole plays and plays
  while people above ground enjoy the music he makes. Excellent illustrations for art
  extensions.

Meyrich, C. (1989). *The musical life of Gustav Mole*. New York: Child's Play International.
Book and cassette: Traces the life of Gustav, a mole, from babyhood to old age. Covers
  many genres of music and a variety of musical instruments. Uses solo, duets, trios,
  quartets, quintets, and a variety of instruments. After a long musical life, Gustav
  becomes an accomplished composer.

copies of the books are available from the library (school librarians
are often willing to order multiple copies for book clubs), each student has his or her own copy. If not enough copies are available for
each member of the group, one student can be selected to read the
story aloud to the other members of the group. After students have
read the text, the group members participate in a discussion. The
discussion leader of the group could be provided with a series of

Table 6.5.   Additional Children's Book Selections Focused on String Music

Carle, E. (1996). *I see a song*. New York: Scholastic.
Celenza, A. (2000). *The farewell symphony*. Watertown, Mass.: Charlesbridge Publishing.
Clement, C. (1989). *The voice of the wood*. New York: Dial.
Ganeri, A. (1996). The young person's guide to the orchestra: Benjamin Britten's composition on CD narrated by Ben Kingsley. San Diego, Calif.: Harcourt Brace.
Gray, L. (1999). *When uncle took the fiddle*. New York: Orchard.
Lambert, P. (1995). *Evening: An Appalachian lullaby*. New York: Roberts Rinehart.
Levine, R. (2000). *Story of the orchestra: A child's introduction to the instruments, the music, the musicians and composers*. New York: Black Dog & Leventhal.
Krull, K. (1993). *Lives of the musicians: Good times, bad times (and what the neighbors thought)*. San Diego, Calif.: Harcourt Brace.
Kuskin, K. (1982). *The philharmonic gets dressed*. New York: HarperCollins.
Moss, L. (1995). *Zin! Zin! Zin! A violin*. New York: Simon and Schuster.
Turner, B. (1996). *The living violin*. New York: Knopf.
Paker, J. (1992). *Music from strings*. Brookfield, Conn.: Milbrook.

questions that can be used as conversation starters. Questions could include some of the following:

- How did the music affect the life of the main character in the book?
- What kind of instruments and music did the characters play?
- Why did the musicians play?
- Who listens to the music in the story and what happens to these listeners?
- How did music change the lives of the characters? How might music change our lives?

In addition to the discussion leader, the music teacher should identify a group member as a scribe who is responsible for making a word and sentence list of the group's answers to the discussion guide. This activity could be co-taught with a classroom teacher so that the students can extend their music book club into classroom language arts time. In addition, the classroom teacher could create a music book center in the classroom for the students to read all of the books during their independent reading time. Additional extensions for the music book club include:

- A performance in which groups dramatize the book's story line and characters with student-created scenery and costumes. These performances could be for younger students at the school site or they could perform for other music classes at the same grade level.

- Music teachers could provide CDs or tape recordings of musical selections appropriate for the student's retelling of the book during language arts time (see table 6.1 for listening selections).
- As a class, with the assistance of the music teacher, students could write their own book incorporating string instruments, music, and musicians (see table 6.5).
- Students could display music book club and journal creations at musical performances throughout the year.

Table 6.6.   Resources for Teachers

Beall, P., and Nipp, S. (1994). *Wee-sing songbooks and CDs.* New York: Price Stern Sloan.

Burz, H., & Marshall, K. (1999). *Performance-based curriculum for music and the visual arts: From knowing to showing.* Thousand Oaks, Calif.: Sage Publications.

Brady, M. (1997). *Dancing hearts: Creative arts with books kids love.* Golden, Colo.: Fulcrum Publishing.

California Department of Education. (1996). *Literature for the visual and performing arts: Kindergarten through grade twelve.* Sacramento, Calif.: Author.

Chambers, J., Hood, M., & Peake, M. (1995). *A work of art: Creative activities inspired by famous artists.* Nashville, Tenn.: Incentive Publications.

Chambers, J., & Hood, M. (1997). *Art for writing: Creative ideas to stimulate written activities.* Nashville, Tenn.: Incentive Publications.

Frohardt, D. (1999). *Teaching art with books kids love: Teaching art appreciation, elements of art, and principles of design with award-winning children's books.* Golden, Colo.: Fulcrum.

Gust, J., & McChesney, J. (1995). *Learning about cultures: Literature, celebrations, games and art activities.* Carthage, Ill.: Teaching and Learning Company.

Henry, S. (1999). *Kids' art works: Creating with color, design, texture and more.* Charlotte, Vt.: Williamson Publishing.

Hierstein, J. (1995). *Art activities from award-winning picture books.* Carthage, Ill.: Teaching and Learning Company.

Larrick, N. (1991). *Let's do a poem! Introducing poetry through listening, singing, chanting, impromptu choral reading, body movement, dance, and dramatization.* New York: Delacort Press.

Levene, D. (1993). *Music through children's literature: Theme and variations.* Englewood, Colo.: Teacher Ideas Press.

Ritter, D. (1991). *Literature-based art activities: Creative art projects inspired by 45 popular children's books: PreK-3.* Cypress, Calif.: Creative Teaching Press.

Schecter, D. (1997). *Science art: Projects and activities that teach science concepts and develop process skills.* New York: Scholastic.

Sterling, M. (1994). *Focus on artists.* Huntington Beach, Calif.: Teacher Created Materials.

Tarlow, E. (1998). *Teaching story elements with favorite books: Creative and engaging activities to explore character, plot, setting, and theme: Grades 1–3.* New York: Scholastic.

Walther, I. (1993). *Vincent van Gogh: Vision and reality.* Germany: Taschen.

Welton, J. (1992). *Eyewitness art: Monet.* New York: Dorling Kindersley.

Additional String Projects

Now that students understand and are interested in string topics, consider some of these follow-up activities:

- Invite string performers from the community to perform in music classes or assemblies. Invite students to write introductions to and reviews of these performances.
- Plan a field trip to a community concert that features string instruments. Again, students should have the knowledge to write reviews of these experiences.
- Invite students to build their own string instruments, create a composition, and perform with these instruments.
- Trace the development and geography about where string instruments existed in ancient and modern civilizations (e.g., Greece, China, Persia, India, Africa, etc.)
- Create a bulletin board display of the unit's activities, including interesting string facts, related literature, pictures of book club performances, pictures of local string musicians, letters to the authors of the children's string-related books, interviews with community string players, etc. Use the cover art of the music book club books for bulletin board displays and for art prompts for the students' illustrated journals about this unit.

As children become comfortable within creative and meaningful introductory listening contexts, important additional goals of an effective active listening program are to "build an aural repertoire that represents a wide range of styles, cultures, and genres of music" that will "lead to greater aesthetic satisfaction through listening" (Campbell and Scott-Kassner, 1995, p. 161). The challenge of teaching musical listening well, and within engaging and stimulating classroom learning environments, requires teachers to investigate additional curriculum materials highly related to these musical goals (see table 6.6). We have nothing less than the love of music at stake.

CONCLUSION

If one of our professional goals is to fully educate children within each of the core curriculum subject areas, we simply cannot ignore the considerable avenues for creative reader response found within the plethora of children's literature about music and art. To do so would be to deprive many of our students the joy of personal, meaningful, and highly creative interaction with quality literature about the arts, artists, and their own artistry. Instead, it should be our goal to develop arts-loving readers within a future where our cultural arts not only survive, but thrive, because they are understood, appreciated, and valued by the many, rather than the few.

Questions for further discussion, study, and project development:

- Why should children's literature be used in integrated arts lessons?
- Select one children's book from each section in this chapter (books about visual artists, books about music and musicians, books about poetry and rhythmic text, books about listening to music, and books about drama and dance) to read, consider, and address the following questions:

  - What suggestions were made for students' creative, expressive responses to this text?
  - What additional ideas do you have?
  - What standards do these learning activities address?
  - How might you use these books in your classroom?

- Select a painting, a recorded piece of music, a dance performance or video, or a performance or video of a play to develop your own unit about arts and artists.

CHAPTER 7

But, I Really Don't Sing, Draw, Paint, Act, or Dance and There's Just No Time, Space, Supplies, Budget, Support, Interest . . .

Develop interest in life as you see it; in people, things, literature, music—the world is so rich, simply throbbing with rich treasures, beautiful souls and interesting people. Forget yourself.

—Henry Miller

In schools across the country, classroom teachers are using integrated arts as a way to ensure that their students access information and gain new understandings of the material presented in class. Unfortunately, far too many classroom teachers do not feel comfortable with integrated arts to attempt this type of lesson in their classroom. These teachers might have been told, as children, to "mouth the words, but don't really sing" because a well-meaning adult wanted the choir to sound perfect. As a result, some teachers are not comfortable with their own artistic ability and are unsure to find resources to assist them. Thankfully, most colleges in the nation offer courses in "arts for teachers," which will provide some of this knowledge for teachers. In addition, most states and school districts offer professional development activities in arts education for teachers. Similarly, several state and national conferences cover this topic (see table 7.4 for national membership organizations).

However, one often-overlooked resource can be found on the school site. Most schools have an arts specialist, typically fine arts or music. We encourage classroom teachers and arts specialists to begin to work together and ensure that our three nonmutually exclusive goals are met:

1. that every student have access to integrated arts education in their classroom;

2. that every student is encouraged to learn with and through the arts by participating in performances, exhibitions, classroom activities, etc. that reinforce the notion that arts permeate life and culture;
3. that students who choose to develop expertise in an art have access to an arts specialist.

The remainder of this chapter focuses on the perspectives and communication needs of classroom teachers and arts specialists (through constructed dialogue and narration), which then evolves into a collaboratively designed performance unit based on the children's literature piece, *Sarah, Plain and Tall* by Patricia MacLachlan (1985). As previously noted, collaboration between classroom teachers and arts specialists is one of the most powerful ways to ensure that every student has access to integrated arts education. The people in this conversation include:

N: Nan, a music specialist
D: Doug, a classroom teacher

A conversation taking place sometime in early October . . .

N: Oh, Hi Doug! Haven't even had a chance to say hello to you! *(anxiously)* I've got three programs to whip together in the next five weeks! Say, could you bring your class ten minutes later on Wednesdays so that I can finish my rehearsals with my instrument ensemble?

D: *(shaking his head)* Noooo . . . that would cut *my* prep time short and really mess up my very packed guided reading group schedule for the morning. I am under a lot of stress to document how I have improved my teaching to ensure that our reading test scores are not below average again. I feel like I have a gun to my head . . . . Even ten minutes will . . .

N: *(interrupting loudly)* Ten minutes? Ten minutes? I have six other classes that day and get behind because most teachers get their kids here late, yet you want me to be done right on time. I have really had it! *(exasperated)* I'm not a jukebox or a program machine, you know!

D: *(wondering why he didn't just walk away before this usual type of conversation with Nan started)* Sorry, I can't help. Hang in there . . .

Later, Doug dramatically recounts this conversation to another classroom teacher. Nan is not present.

D: *(sarcastically)* Nan is always so stressed, so completely focused on her own performances. I wish my worst problem was twenty kids on little instruments, practicing the same songs over and over again! She has no test scores to worry about and only one subject to teach. She doesn't know what it's like to have total responsibility for students and worry about what their parents think about school.

Later, Nan dramatically recounts the original conversation with Doug to another music specialist in her district. Doug is not present.

N: *(angrily)* I have to work with completely narrow-minded people. Don't they know that our kids need more than higher test scores and teachers who teach the tests? They don't know how music connects to everything they do. I would drop dead if even three of the teachers showed any interest in my curriculum!

Communication problems of this nature continue for years. Resentment builds to a breaking point. Nan only speaks to some classroom teachers when she thinks they need to negotiate their schedules for her rehearsal needs. Doug views Nan as the rather melodramatic and needy teacher, who provides him a much needed break—a chance for his own preparation and paperwork. Neither Nan or Doug listen to each other or attempt to articulate the hidden issues—what each might say if given the opportunity in a safe, respectful environment. If given the chance, each of these teachers might say something like the following:

D: I'm sick of my students having to leave all of the time for "specials" like music and art. I don't see any connection to the things that I'm teaching. For example, I was recently teaching a unit on the Lewis and Clark expedition. The music teacher was having the students play recorders on some thing called "Fais, do, do" and the art teacher was stuck on Monet waterlily scenes! Each of these "special" teachers lives in their own world and expects to just get perfect kids who really want to play and paint along. Give me a break!

I wish that they knew more about my curriculum. I know that Nan could offer a lot to my students beyond music. I see other people collaborate; I wonder if it would be possible to collaborate with her? I wonder if she would like to come into my classroom and help me plan my lessons? I know a lot about social studies and language, but I bet she has resources that I don't even know about. We could share responsibility for student achievement. I could even go into her music class and let the students know that I think music is important and that I expect their behavior to be outstanding. I wonder if she wants me in her class. I wonder if she'd like to come into my classroom. If she came into my classroom, I might even be brave enough to sing with my students. I wouldn't try to sing now, but with help, I might.

N: I'm sick of the constant adaptation I have to do to accommodate all other teachers and subjects at this school. No one helps me out, though. It is as though expected programs are everything, yet I am supposed to perform miracles and get the kids ready without anyone else adjusting their needs. You guys (classroom teachers) don't have to get up there

with every kid in the school and have the performance be the single in-
dicator of how well you teach music! I have every child in this school—
some for six years in a row. I don't get to pass my discipline nightmares
on to the next teacher! My schedule, working conditions, noise problems, and program expectations are not of my choosing, you know . . . I
resent being an entertainer. I have a curriculum and standards to teach
and assess. My class is not recess. I wish I could actually get through the
curriculum that I have planned. I am a teacher, too!

I need you to take an interest in your students' musical development.
I'd like your help and suggestions. Maybe we could work together and
take some pressure off of all of us? Come to your kids' music class five
minutes before they leave so we can share with you what we are learning. I'd love to hear what you think. . . .

Maybe we could create some musical connections to what you are doing in your classroom. Ask me about all my song materials, CDs, videos,
dances, and literature. Do some of our activities reinforce your existing
curricular needs? I have a lot of theme ideas, especially in connection to
children's literature and social studies. *We music teachers are a walking
embodiment of a rich tradition of history and culture through song.* I'll bet
I have some ideas that could help you out. Could we work together? I
need help in viewing my job as much more than performance preparation.

A MUSIC SPECIALIST AND A CLASSROOM TEACHER MEET

The goals of each of these teachers are similar: to advance the knowledge of children. Each brings a unique perspective to the classroom.
Are collaborations between classroom teachers and music teachers really possible? What would the outcome of such collaboration look like?
As teachers, we have had the opportunity to collaborate on unit and lesson design. One such unit focused on Westward expansion, a social
studies theme commonly found within upper elementary curriculum.

The trade book for our unit was *Sarah, Plain and Tall* (MacLachlan,
1985), a Newbery Award-winning book. The Newbery Award is given
each year to the best work in children's literature (*Sarah, Plain and Tall*
was also made into a Hallmark Hall of Fame, made-for-TV film starring
Glen Close). This book is also on core reading lists in most states. We selected this book because it met our criteria for quality children's literature (e.g., Fisher, Lapp, and Flood, 1999) and its potential connections to
social studies and the arts. Our overriding goal was for our students to
better understand this historical period through immersion into the Sarah
story, and the songs and dances that were popular during this era. As we
planned this unit, we discussed our "nonnegotiables." These included:

- music thoughtfully integrated within the unit (not just as a background activity).
- a rich variety of related children's literature and poetry to extend this thematic focus.
- increased comprehension of content material (song text, poems, books, and other print material) by integrating the curriculum, movement, arts, and literacy activities.
- enhanced motivation through direct participation.
- a culminating activity or informal performance blending songs and dances of this historical period with a dramatization of the text *Sarah, Plain and Tall*.

Although Jacobs (1989, 1997) has identified several ways in which disciplines can be combined, we planned our lessons within an integrated thematic unit. By this we mean that learning in each discipline requires the use of knowledge from the other disciplines under study. Curricular integration of this sort is not merely a superficial or clever usage of a popular educational buzzword, but rather a purposeful focus of a rich variety of learning activities designed to enhance the child's active learning. According to the National Standards in Music (1994b):

> Ultimately the outcomes of schooling must cut across subject-matter fields in order to be useful. Each of the arts must maintain its integrity in the curriculum and be taught of its own sake, but at the same time the curriculum should emphasize relationships among the arts and relationships between the arts and disciplines outside the arts. Music can serve as a particularly useful framework within which to teach a wide array of skills and knowledge, particularly in social studies and language arts. (MENC, 1994b, p. 4)

With these purposes in mind, we sat down in Doug's classroom and began our collaboration on *Sarah, Plain and Tall*. We knew his upcoming social studies unit was westward expansion.

> **N:** I just had an idea. Because *Sarah, Plain and Tall* is in the voice of women, men, and children moving West during the 1800s, and expresses a lot of words and feelings found in American folk songs of that time . . . do you see a possible connection? There must be a lot of songs in our music text from that period of time that would be very appropriate to use with *Sarah, Plain and Tall*. Wouldn't it be great to have our students read, dramatize dialogues from the book, and interject music and song text from that period? Song texts are poetry and wouldn't always need to be sung, but could be used as spoken, dramatized poetry for your language arts lessons.

D: *(thrilled!)* Wow, we're getting some good ideas here! Your *Sarah, Plain and Tall* ideas meet our school's focus on integrated curriculum. They also provide me a new way to teach comprehension—imagine the understanding we could create with this sustained study! Songs and dramatic readings might encourage a different level of reader response (Rosenblatt, 1995) and have a greater impact on understanding (Cox and Many, 1992). Would I know any of the songs you're talking about? How about on page 15 of *Sarah, Plain and Tall* . . . Sarah, who is a mail-order bride for a mid-1800s Midwestern homestead widower with two young children, writes a letter to her potential husband and family, saying simply ". . . tell them I sing." So, what would she be singing? Do you know the song Sarah sings in the book, "Sumer is icumen in?" *(Nan nods).* Could you come in to our classroom as we read aloud and teach us that song and others from the book's historical time period?

N: *(Nan thinks to herself, "Interesting . . . . "Sumer is icumen in" is Old English. How did Sarah come to know that song? She grew up in coastal Maine . . . I wonder how she came to know this song?)* Sure Doug, we could even have our music class in your classroom. Or you could come to our music class and learn the songs with the kids. I'll give you the song copies and CD recordings so you can use them in your classroom during language arts (see table 7.1 for a list of appropriate music sources). Also, I have ideas for listening to music that can be used with *Sarah, Plain and Tall.*

D: *(interrupting, excitedly).* That's great! Especially if I have a CD to help me. As part of our Western movement unit, the kids and I will read aloud *Sarah, Plain and Tall*, probably within five consecutive days. I was thinking that I could have students reenact our read-aloud each day in small-group dramatic scenes. For instance, it would be interesting to see how our students would enact the dialogue and narrative ideas from chapter 3, when the children in the book meet Sarah. Tell me what kind of music you suggest as scene setters within some chapter groupings.

N: Okay, I'll look at the book again. I will try to read it through your eyes.

D: I have some art prints of a painter's works of coastal Maine (Sarah's homeland) and of pioneer themes of the 1800s. I think that I have some poetry from that period also. Another book, *Miss Rumphius* (Cooney, 1982) has some of the exact themes found in *Sarah, Plain and Tall*—an independent woman who longs to live by the sea and all her memories of growing up in coastal New England. I know another book that could really be appealing to younger kids, *The Seashore Book* (Zolotow, 1992). The text is very poetic and could even be used to add to the narrative about Sarah's memories of the seashore. It is full of absolutely beautiful illustrations and expressive text! You feel like you are at the shore.

I have a lot of other books in my classroom library (see table 7.2 for sources) and some teacher resource books about integrated curriculum based on children's literature (see table 7.3 for resources).

Table 7.1.   Music Sources for the Westward Expansion Unit

Song Title	Grade, TE pg, CD#
Sumer is acumen in (Sarah's song)	5, pg. 316, CD 12–22
Cumberland Gap	3, pg. 248, CD 8–30
	4, pg. 255, CD 9–40
Old Joe Clark	5, pg. 307, CD 12–13
Shenandoah	8, pg. 125, CD 6–3
Oh, Susanna	4, pg. 172, CD 7–9
This Land is Your Land	3, pg. 116, CD 4–23
Clementine	4, pg. 169, CD 7–7
Barb'ry Allen	6, pg. 261, CD 10–22
Simple Gifts	8, pg. 158, CD 6–29
Amazing Grace	4, pg. 302, CD 10–36
	5, pg. 104, CD 5–4
America, the Beautiful	3, pg. 185, CD 6–22 thru 24
Sweet Betsy from Pike	4, pg. 166, CD 7–6
Skip to My Lou	3, pg. 43, CD 2–17
Wreck of the Edmund Fitzgerald	4, pg. 152, CD 6–15
Poem:	
"Song of the Sea Wind"	4, pg. 135, CD 5–27
Instrumental Music Recordings:	
"Old Joe Clark"	2, pg. 22, CD 1–22
"I Bought me a Cat"	K pg. 199, CD 5–4
"Cripple Creek" fiddle tune	4, pg. 23, CD 1–20

Source: Silver, Burdett, & Ginn (1995) *The Music Connection*. Parsippany, N.J.: Silver, Burdett, & Ginn.

N: Maybe we could use *Miss Rumphius* and other children's literature and poetry to surround the Sarah theme. Wow, can I borrow those art prints and the other books? They would be great when I'm introducing the songs we're going to do for this unit. We could use the art as prompts for our students' journal writing during music-listening lessons. Did I ever tell you that your students have been compiling listening journals for the past two years?

D: What? They have? How do they write about music? I'd like to read them!

N: Oh yeah, haven't I told you? It's part of how I meet standards in music, particularly those involving listening, analyzing, and describing music *(National Standard #6)*.

D: *(pause)* Boy, our students are really going to benefit by understanding the context of the book and the arts of the time period in which it was set. But . . . I was wondering, how do we get closure on this integrated unit? I know my students. They want to know where this whole thing is going.

N: Hmmm . . . How about some kind of informal presentation of *Sarah, Plain and Tall* as our culminating project? Our students could

Table 7.2.   Children's Literature Sources

Cooney, B. (1982). *Miss Rumphius*. New York: Viking Press.

King, D. C. (1997). *Pioneer days: Discover the past with fun projects, games, activities and recipes*. New York: Wiley.
Ages 9–12. Adventures of a brother and sister living on the frontier in 1843. Forty fun projects, wealth of historical information and illustrations.

Cushman, K. (1998). *The ballad of Lucy Whipple*. New York: HarperCollins.
Ages 9–12. Girl uprooted to California mining camp called "Lucky Diggins" in the Sierra. Lucy grows and changes in her new environment . . . packed with more history than history books. She wrote letters to her grandmother in Massachusetts about hating her new environment. Lucy is an avid reader and grows up to become a librarian.

Gregory, K. (1997). *Across the wide and lonesome prairie: The Oregon Trail diary of Hattie Campbell (Dear America)*. New York: Scholastic.
In the voice of 13-year-old Hattie, the 1847 Oregon Trail wagon train is explained.

Zolotow, C. (1992). *The seashore book*. New York: HarperCollins.
Richly illustrated and poetic text about a mother explaining in beautiful, poetic prose, the sights, sounds, smells and feel of her beloved seashore to her son who has only lived in the mountains. Highly connected to Sarah's childhood on the Maine seashore.

Werner, E. (1996). *Pioneer children on the journey west*. New York: HarperCollins.
Voices, diaries, journals, memoirs of 120 young immigrants, ages 4–17. Stories from the Missouri river to Pacific Ocean 1841–1865, in the voice of young people. This book assists in students' understanding of Sarah's life.

Curtis, J., Curtis, W., Lieberman, F., and Little, C. (1995). *Monhegan, the Artists' Island*. New York: Down East Books.
Features the Maine islands' famous artist residents—Rockwell Kent, Robert Henri, George Bellows, Edward Hopper, and Andrew and Jamie Wyeth.

Table 7.3.   Teacher Resources: Curriculum Integration

Note to teachers: These are excellent resources for integrating the arts into units based on children's literature. Sources include art projects, poetry, creative drama ideas, music connections, and performance suggestions for both music specialists and classroom teachers.

Tarlow, E. (1998). *Teaching story elements with favorite books*. New York: Scholastic.
Levene, D. B. (1993). *Music through children's literature: Theme and variations*. Englewood, Colo.: Teacher Idea Press.
Hierstein, J. (1995). *Art activities from award-winning picture books*. Carthage, Ill.: Teaching and Learning Company.

share their new knowledge with younger or older students in one of our classrooms, rather than the auditorium! Our students could design some simple scenery and sets for each of the chapters in different areas of the room. Students could be selected to narrate the progression of the story between performed scenes. Songs and dances could be incorporated into the presentation and story action between chapters to connect the story to the musical life of the people of the times.

We could display the artwork that the students did in their illustrations of the book's scenes, as well as the prints of the artist's works of this historical period. We could also display the students' renditions and reinterpretations of the book chapters and their music listening journals. You know, it might become a *Sarah, Plain and Tall* interactive museum! We could even have the students bring in Americana antiques and farm artifacts. Students could then serve as tour guides, or "docents" through the Sarah exhibit!

D: Yes, and you know that page 15 thing I mentioned, when Sarah writes "tell them I sing?" We could have the Sarah character actually sing "Sumer is icumen in" and talk to the audience about the origins of her song. How old is that song, where did it come from, and what do those strange words mean? Why would Sarah know that song? Great discovery learning potential.

N: Why not! Would you mind if right after we perform this integrated unit in your classroom, we do it again in my spring concert for parents? You could help me narrate why and how we created this integrated music, art, drama, social studies, and language arts unit. We could even have the students display their "Sarah" museum and serve as docents to the parents. I think the parents might see much more of our creative integrated teaching and learning than they would by just sitting through a concert of ten pieces of music. I think we're on to something with these themes units. Can I tell some of the other teachers about this?

D: Sure . . . I have a whole year of literature themes to share with you! You know, after we learn about Westward expansion, we could focus on the California and Alaska gold rushes! What do you know about that?

AFTERTHOUGHT

Positive changes in our relationships with our teaching colleagues can result in creative curriculum collaborations and rewarding teaching and learning experiences for our students. Within this article's constructed dialogue, we have modeled the solicitation of a peer's ideas and strengths, content, and teaching expertise. Simply put, the teachers in this story asked and listened, and eventually delighted in each other's perspective. Through these dialogical actions, the article's conversation traced the development of a type of informed empathy. As Deborah Meier (1996) reminds us:

Democratic society depends on our openness to other ideas, our willingness to suspend belief long enough to entertain ideas contrary to our own, and the expectation that our ideas are forever "in progress," unfinished, and incomplete. But, it also depends on our developing the habit of stepping in the shoes of others—both intellectually and emotionally. (p. 272)

We encourage you to invite your colleagues to take a similar risk—knock on doors and invite them to share and exchange their teaching expertise—"Tell them I sing."

Questions for further discussion, study, and project development:

- Which arts do you feel comfortable doing, making, or leading? Why?
- Which arts do you not feel comfortable doing, making, or leading? Why?
- Interview either an arts specialist or a classroom teacher (depending on your own job responsibilities) and ask him or her about integrated arts education and opportunities for collaboration between arts specialists and classroom teachers.
- Why would you advocate for all students to receive integrated arts instruction in their classroom?
- Why would you advocate for all students to have opportunities to learn through the arts by participating in arts and arts performances?
- Why would you argue for students who choose to develop specific expertise in arts to have access to an arts specialist?

Project idea:

E-mail, write, or call the following Arts organizations for information about their work (see table 7.4):

Table 7.4.   Arts Membership Organizations

The following organizations provide a wealth of resources, teacher inservices, and publications toward your efforts in developing arts-loving readers:

American Alliance for Theatre and Education
Arizona State University Theatre Department
P.O. Box 872002
Tempe, Ariz. 85287-2002
(602) 965-6064
http://www.aate.com/welcome.htm

American Orff-Schulwerk Association (Music and Movement for Children)
http://www.aosa.org

Association for Supervision and Curriculum Development
1703 N. Beauregard St.
Alexandria, Va. 22311-1714
(800) 933-2723
http://www.ascd.org

The California Arts Project
P.O. Box 4925
San Rafael, Calif. 94913
(415) 499-5893
http://www.csmp.ucop.edu/tcap/

Educational Theatre Association
3368 Central Parkway
Cincinnati, Ohio 45225
(513) 559-1996
http://www.etassoc.org/

The Getty Center for Education in the Arts
401 Wilshire Boulevard, Suite 950
Santa Monica, Calif. 90401-1455
(310) 395-6657
http://www.getty.edu/artsednet/

The John F. Kennedy Center for the Performing Arts
Washington, D.C. 20566-0001
(800) 444-1324
http://www.kennedy-center.org/

Metropolitan Museum of Art
http://www.metmuseum.org/
MENC: The National Association for Music Education
1806 Robert Fulton Drive
Reston, Va. 22091
(703) 860-4000
http://www.menc.org

National Art Education Association
1916 Association Drive
Reston, Va. 22091
(703) 860-8000
http://www.naea-reston.org

National Dance Association
1900 Association Drive
Reston, Va. 22091-1502
(703) 476-3436
http://www.aahperd.org/nda/ndda.html

National Endowment for the Arts
Nancy Hanks Center
1100 Pennsylvania Avenue NW
Washington, D.C. 20506-0001
(202) 682-5400
http://arts.endow.gov/

National Endowment for the Humanities
1100 Pennsylvania Avenue NW
Washington, D.C. 20506
(202) 606-8400

Table 7.4.   (continued) Arts Membership Organizations

http://www.neh.fed.us/
Scott Foresman Publishing/Silver, Burdett, & Ginn Music
Publisher for *Music Connection* (1995, 2000) and *Making Music* (2002)
http://www.scottforesman.com
Select Silver Burdett Ginn Music

Smithsonian Museum
http://www.si.edu

CHAPTER 8

This Won't Work with My Class . . .

Once social change begins, it cannot be reversed. You cannot un-educate the person who has learned to read. You cannot humiliate the person who feels pride. You cannot oppress the people who are not afraid anymore.

—Cesar Chavez

HOW CAN DIVERSE LEARNERS PARTICIPATE IN INTEGRATED ARTS LESSONS?

The schools of the twenty-first century bustle with the promise of the future, a future enriched by the diversity of today's students. An exuberant mix of cultures and languages, abilities, and talents weaves a tapestry of learning in classrooms that maximize this potential. As with all great possibilities, there is the shadow of failure as well. Schools with diverse student populations, particularly many urban schools, face challenges that mirror the difficulties of the larger society: hunger and neglect, low expectations and even lower self-image, division, and marginalization. Schools have long been viewed as the emergency room of society—a place where the ills of the community are to be bandaged and treated. But triage is not teaching, and treatment is not learning.

The population of a school reflects the community, and its classrooms should as well. The diversity of a school is most often viewed through the three lenses: students with disabilities, English language learners, and students identified as gifted or talented. These students bring to the classroom their unique talents, as well as their support needs. In the past, the prevailing practice was to isolate these learners into discrete groups, in the mistaken belief that a specialized system of supports could then be implemented. However, decades of research have proven that the outcomes didn't match the promises.

STUDENTS WITH DISABILITIES

Students with disabilities, including those with learning disabilities, physical disabilities, and behavioral disabilities, have historically encountered barriers to equity and excellence in their school experience. Although public schools were designed to provide free and appropriate public education for all students, those identified with disabilities have not always received the same type of education, including arts instruction, as their peers without disabilities. A continuum of placements was designed to provide a full range of services for individuals with disabilities, from the most restrictive to the least-restrictive environments. At one time, it was common practice to place individuals with disabilities that required the most intense services in the most restrictive environment, separating them from their same-age peers (U.S. Department of Education, 1999). Educators now see that separate education often results in social exclusion in school and the community, acquisition of inappropriate behavior, and an inability to generalize knowledge to new environments (Yell, Rogers, and Rogers, 1998). Further, students without disabilities grew up without the experience of knowing peers with disabilities, leaving them ill-prepared to become friends, neighbors, employers, co-workers, parents of individuals with disabilities, or individuals with disabilities themselves (Fisher, Pumpian, and Sax, 1998). Thus, inclusive education has become part of many school-reform efforts, impacting not only schools, but also the community (Kennedy and Fisher, 2001).

An inclusive education offers students with disabilities the opportunity to apply functional skills in the general education classroom while also accessing the curriculum standards alongside their peers. Inclusion is typically thought of as the placement of students with disabilities in their neighborhood schools in general education classrooms with peers their own age (NASBE, 1995). Caution must be taken to provide appropriate supports and services in these classrooms for students to be included, versus letting them be "dumped" without support. This includes the tendency of "dumping" students with disabilities in arts classes because these classes were perceived as less rigorous and there was no other way to address the goal of mainstreaming. Coordinating supports and accommodations is necessary for success; indeed, we owe it to all students.

ENGLISH LANGUAGE LEARNERS

In terms of English language learners, we know that many students who are learning English as a second language do not receive their education in a bilingual classroom or from a bilingual teacher. This could be because of the lack of available personnel, the number of students representing the specific language group, or pressures from politicians and public debate (August and Hakuta, 1998). As a result, many students who are learning English are educated in the "low" group and spend a significant amount of their instructional time with remedial work (Dugan and Desir, 1998). Fortunately, there is a great deal of information available about instruction for English language learners in mainstream classes (e.g., Faltis and Wolfe, 1998; Watts-Taffe and Truscott, 2000). Although not replacing the need for quality bilingual education, students who are learning English and who are enrolled in content classes require support to be successful. The types of instructional support necessary include many of the ideas included in the remainder of this chapter.

STUDENTS WHO ARE ACADEMICALLY GIFTED AND TALENTED

Students identified as gifted have benefited from excellent instruction; the failed promise is in who has been excluded, and in the damage done to a school community when students are separated from their peers. In gifted education, outstanding curriculum design approaches have been developed and implemented, including differentiated instruction (Tomlinson, 1999) and multiple intelligences (Gardner, 1993a, b). But traditional gifted education approaches have failed to overcome the underrepresentation of African Americans (Ford, 1998; Harris and Ford, 1999; Sisk, 1994), Hispanics and Latinos (Strom, 1990), Native Americans (Romero, 1994), English language learners (Peterson and Margolin, 1997), students with disabilities (Baum, Olenchak, and Owen, 1998; Hiatt and Covington, 1991), and gender (Sadker, 1999). And most educators are in agreement that these students are most at-risk, and most in need of excellent supports. Doesn't it make sense then that well-designed curricular supports are made available to all students, thus circumventing this history of underrepresentation?

School communities suffer as well when students identified as gifted are singled out for special and often inequitable education. A powerful and destructive message is conveyed to all students when a school endorses the blatant hierarchy of competitive achievement that pits one student against another (Sapon-Shevin, 1994a). As Sapon-Shevin (1994b) notes, separate, "gifted-only" classes disrupt the sense of community on a school campus and serves as a continual reminder of each individual's worth.

The fields of special education, second-language acquisition, and gifted education offer excellent supports for all learners, not just those identified as possessing a set of characteristics. We believe the answer to the focus question for this chapter is simple—teachers ensure that their diverse learners participate in quality instruction. Thus, the remainder of this chapter focuses on instructional strategies—instructional strategies that teachers can use to engage all of their students, including those who are identified as gifted and talented, English language learners, and students with disabilities. We would like to point out that no teacher uses all of these instructional strategies in a given lesson. Rather, teachers pick and choose instructional strategies, based on the content to be covered, the materials available, the students' needs, and their goals for the lesson.

REALIA

Imagine that you have never seen a violin or heard an orchestra. How difficult would this lack of experience make your understanding of the book *The Cello of Mr. O* (see chapter 6)? Realia provides learners with an example of the topic or word under study (Lapp, Fisher, and Flood, 1999). Realia can be authentic photos, tangible items, or replications of distinct parts of a larger item. For example, science teachers often use human skeletons to discuss the human bone structure. Science teachers might also use photographs, images, drawings, or plastic models of the brain and central nervous system. Often, teachers use authentic period music as realia for social studies lessons. Regardless of the specific type of realia, these items build the learners' confidence in their language abilities, makes language learning more relevant, contextualizes the learning, and prepares learners for post-classroom experiences.

TOTAL PHYSICAL RESPONSE (TPR)

Total Physical Response (TPR) is a language development methodology based on the coordination of speech and action developed by James Asher (1996). TPR has been in use for nearly thirty years. While other methods have come and gone, TPR is still a valuable tool when teaching English language learners (and others for whom language is difficult such as students with learning disabilities). Despite the wealth of materials available to us, nothing is more useful than this very direct and visual instruction.

With the TPR method, the teacher says a single action word or phrase such as "stand up" or "put the paper on the table" and then demonstrates the action. At first, students will only be able to follow the command. They might also be able to repeat the teacher's words as they copy the action. The next step is to proceed to more difficult language while still keeping the instruction direct and visual. Many teachers use simple TPR sequences in order to enlarge the students' vocabulary, teach the present continuous and past tense in context, and practice English sentence structure and word order.

For example, a teacher might use TPR to provide instructions for a learning center by audio recording the instructions with background music. This gives the teacher the opportunity to repeat the instructions, demonstrate the action, and not worry about what command to do next. The teacher can then be sure that he or she has covered all of the actions required. This tape recorder method also helps the teacher maintain a record of what has been done. Of course, teachers can save the tapes, share them with colleagues, and use them again with new groups of students.

SCAFFOLDING INSTRUCTION: SHOW, TELL, QUESTION, AND CLARIFY

Scaffolding is the practice of following an instructional sequence to better aid learning. A typical sequence that teachers build into their lesson plans includes (Wilkinson and Silliman, 2000):

- *explicit modeling*, usually in the form of a demonstration of a strategy or task.
- *direct explanations* of the strategy or task they have just shared, including the theoretical framework.
- *eliciting student response* by asking questions and probing for students' construction of meaning.
- *verifying and clarifying* through further questioning so that any misinformation can be corrected.

This practice echoes Vygotsky's (1978) theory of "zones of proximal development." Vygotsky theorized that when learners receive support just beyond what they can accomplish independently, they learn new skills and concepts.

Many teachers have translated this pattern to show, tell, question, and clarify as a way to utilize scaffolding in the introduction of new material. A lesson in a science class demonstrates this pattern. The class had been studying the spread of diseases in the Middle Ages, some of it because of poor hygiene and medical care. The teacher set up a lab for students to examine common bacteria using microscopes. She began by showing the students what they would be doing using a video microscope hooked up to her computer and projected on a screen, thereby allowing all the students to view the prepared slides at $4x$, $10x$, and $40x$ powers. She then proceeded to tell about the three objective lenses of the microscope. Next, she questioned students about the advantages and disadvantages of each lens power. Finally, she clarified some of the misinformation she heard, including Paul's suggestion that the $40x$ lens would be the best way to locate an object on a slide. She began the show, tell, question, and clarify sequence again by demonstrating the difficulties of using the $40x$ lens for that purpose. The teacher later commented that showing students first seems to be more useful because students are able to ask higher-order questions because many of the procedural details have been demonstrated already.

The haiku lesson in chapter 4 also demonstrates this model. First the teacher demonstrated her haiku performance. She then provided direct explanations of the haiku poetry form and encouraged students to ask questions. She then allowed students to perform the haiku and write their own haiku—thus providing her a way to verify and clarify any misinformation about this format of poetry.

COMPACTING

In compacting, students are assessed on their prior knowledge. Those students who already know the material are assigned other tasks, such as peer tutoring, art projects, library research, and math labs. This allows teachers to focus their lessons on the students who really need it. Two rules guide her use of this strategy. First, the preassessment changes every week. One week it might be paper and pencil, the next could be small group, the next could be oral, and the following week could include a performance. Second, all students must take the final assessment of the material and their grade is based on that score. Teachers like to offer compacting to students because it serves two purposes. In addition to creating an in-class tutoring system, some of the students who are eligible for "compacting out" decide not to because they know that they will perform better on assessments when they participate in the lesson.

INDEPENDENT PROJECTS

Growing numbers of teachers believe that work done outside of school should be interesting and should require students to work with at least one other person. These teachers are most interested in independent projects (previously called *homework*) that requires students to interact with their families and friends. They are least interested in independent projects that encourage students to sit in their bedroom by themselves. We also like independent projects that are challenging for students, but not frustrating.

One example of this comes from a unit on the Middle Ages. A middle school social studies teacher developed several independent projects based on this theme of the Middle Ages. Not all of his students do the same project each night—some students interviewed their elder family members on how the role of children had changed in their lifetime, other students worked together outside of school to film an I-Movie using the school's digital camera (I-Movie software allows students to easily film and edit, and then add special effects and titles). Others explored the paintings, architecture, clothing, and music of the Middle Ages and created poster-board displays of their findings. Others built a model of a medieval town while still others wrote a script for and performed a docudrama on life in the Middle Ages.

CONCEPT MAPS AND CHARACTER WEBS

Visual representations of complex ideas help students organize information. Developing concept or semantic maps is one strategy used by teachers because it provides insights about students' knowledge about the topic. Typically, the main idea is placed in the center of the paper with a small circle drawn around it. Then lines are drawn from the circle to ideas that connect with the main idea. As you can imagine, there can be several subideas to a main idea, and each subidea can have branches of ideas. For example, a class studying transportation could use a concept map to link different types of transportation by the mode (sea, air, land, etc.). Students can be asked to list vehicles under each type: trucks, cars, buses, taxis, and motorcycles could all be placed under the subtopic of land. Some teachers also use concept maps near the end of the unit, typically completed in groups of four, as a way to review for tests. Not only can students review information this way, but the teacher can gain insights about areas that students might not understand.

Some teachers use character webs to focus students' thinking on characters found in literature or other forms of text. One teacher read aloud the chapter book *The Door in the Wall* (De Angeli, 1989), a story about a young English boy who acquires a disability and is abandoned by the superstitious servants who were charged with caring for him. Each student was given a simple drawing of a person's head. As they learned more about Robin (the main character in the book), the students illustrated the simple drawing and placed key words around the head to describe him. Teachers often find that character webs help all students understand character development and are often pleased to find that their students' understanding of the text and character development significantly improves when they are required to create character webs. Character webs could be easily used to analyze live performances in plays or concerts, as well as the subjects of a painting or other work of art. In addition to concept maps, teachers often supplement the visual images of characters with clip art, videos, and computer Web sites to assist students in creating visual representations.

WRITING PROMPTS AND QUESTIONS

Another helpful comprehension strategy is to invite students to create a series of questions to answer as they read textbooks and informational texts. This could be as simple as having students read the end-of-chapter questions prior to and throughout the reading of the chapter. Some students will consider this "cheating" when their teachers first suggest it and need to be assured that using questions in advance is a strategy that effective readers often use. Focusing on the questions helps students chunk, summarize, and synthesize the newly acquired information. When there are no "end-of-unit" questions, students should create questions that focus their reading. These questions are often first developed during the "what I want to learn" part of the KWL (Ogle, 1986, 1996) or by changing text subheadings into questions.

During writing assignments, students often perform better when the prompt is changed from a question into a sentence starter. For example, instead of asking students to respond to a question like "What is the role of a vassal?" the phrase could be re-written to read, "The role of a vassal is to . . ." Additional examples she developed include: "The economic effect of the Black Death was . . ." and "The Moors' influence on European learning included . . ." or "Common subjects of medieval art include . . ." This format for questioning is especially effective for English language learners, who sometimes struggle with interrogatives in a new language.

TIERED ASSIGNMENTS AND TESTS

Many teachers have found that, when students have choice in their assignments, they perform better. For this reason, some teachers provide a full page of assignments that students can complete for class. Each assignment is worth a maximum number of points and students select which assignments to complete, based on their interests. Although other teachers have different rules regarding tiered assignments, some let students do as many assignments as they want in order to earn the grade that they want.

In addition to the tiered assignments, teachers can use tiered tests to increase participation and choice in the curriculum. These type of end-of-unit tests typically have five parts: true/false, multiple choice, short answer, short essay with illustration, and long essay. Teachers often like for their students to have experience with different ways of demonstrating their knowledge so that they will do well on the statewide assessments. One example of tiered tests illustrates the possibilities. A math teacher uses a five-part tiered test. During test time, students are required to complete any two sections of the test. When he returns the test the following day, he has graded the two sections that each student completed. The students then complete one additional section of the test—again, their choice. This math teacher does this for several reasons. First, students can demonstrate their knowledge the best way they know how. Second, students learn to use the test as a tool. That is, there are answers to questions in other questions on a test. Third, students talk about the test during passing periods and lunch after the first administration. Although the students think they are being sly, the teacher likes that they are using their time to talk about the curriculum. Finally, he likes that these tests communicate to students that knowledge is never complete—there is always more to know and learn.

PERFORMING AS A WAY TO LEARN

As suggested in other parts of this book, we believe that comprehension is enhanced with drama, music, and movement. Children who struggle with concepts of character development, sequence, and motivation can experience the stories in other ways when performance techniques are used. For example, teachers can use a Reader's Theatre strategy in which students assume the roles of characters and recreate the dialogue from the text. Viewers follow along in the text to reinforce their own skills.

Students may also be encouraged to demonstrate their knowledge through creative, integrated arts applications including the following:

- Writing, acting, and directing a scripted interpretation of a book, historical event, vignette, or biographical incident
- Learning and performing songs, dances, and musical pieces appropriate for the unit of study
- Making and displaying their own art projects, which interpret the unit of study
- Writing and performing their own poetry with expressive speech and movement sequences

FLEXIBLE GROUPING

Classroom instruction in the United States has been traditionally characterized by permanent homogeneous-ability groups constituted by teacher assessment of student achievement. Research conducted during the past two decades has indicated that permanent ability grouping can create serious social and emotional problems for students. As a result, teachers attempt to implement more flexible grouping patterns, which accommodate the interplay of ideas among students. We believe that teachers should feel comfortable using many types of grouping patterns for many different purposes. For example, whole-class instruction is useful when teachers have short bits of information to convey to students, such as the causes of World War II, or when reinforcing a skill or strategy. Whole-class instruction is also useful during the learning of songs, demonstrations of art techniques, and group choreography. However, whole-class instruction is not the only way to teach arts activities.

In addition to whole-class homogeneous grouping, teachers can use flexible grouping patterns to meet the needs of their increasingly diverse student population. Grouping patterns that are flexible provide teachers an opportunity to observe students working in a variety of situations, including working alone, partners working together, and small cooperative teams working and creating together.

We believe that students should experience three types of groups every week: teacher-selected groups, student-selected groups, and random groups. During teacher selected group time, teachers can use

CARS (Center Activity Rotation System) (Lapp, Flood, and Goss, 2000). Within this rotation system, students are divided into heterogeneous cooperative groups. Each of the groups works at a learning center that is related to the theme that the whole class is studying. In addition to the heterogeneous groups, the teacher works with specific students at a teacher center. The teacher can select specific students each day to work within small teacher-led groups that focus on a specific skill or information that needs direct, explicit teaching. To ensure that all students receive small-group instruction, the teachers should meet with each student during center rotations. Let's look at a few of the centers that one teacher used to teach her students about the Civil War.

One center involves fraction quilts. This center requires students to apply their math knowledge and re-create quilts similar to those made by slaves during Civil War times. Another center focuses on writing. At this center, students begin their biographies. Students understand the task because the whole class has been reading biographies about people who lived during the Civil War. At a third center, students view a film about life during the Civil War. The teacher wants to ensure that her students have a visual understanding of the life and times of American history. She also wants to ensure that her students who are less fluent in English have a visual representation of the vocabulary that the class is discussing. At the next center, students meet to discuss the text that the whole class is reading. They also record their responses and predictions to share later in the day during the teacher read-aloud. At another center, students read independently from narrative and nonnarrative books. This center reinforces the importance of reading and supplements the free-choice reading, which students do daily. As with all of her lessons in which she uses CARS, there is a teacher center. The teacher meets with different groups each day, which allows her to address specific skills needs and to assess her student's learning.

In addition to these teacher-selected groups, teachers design lessons in which students select their own groups. This often happens during independent projects or library research. Finally, teachers use random groups to ensure that students have the opportunity to interact with everyone in the class. One of our favorite ways to do this is with playing cards. Each student gets a card and then all the students who have the same number meet. This strategy also allows for a natural regrouping when the students report in groups of diamonds, hearts, spades, and clubs.

ACCOMMODATIONS AND MODIFICATIONS

Accommodations and modifications are techniques used by special educators to ensure that students with disabilities can access the core curriculum in general education classrooms (e.g., Fisher, Frey, and Sax, 1999). An *accommodation* is a change made to the teaching or testing procedures in order to provide a student with access to information and to create an equal opportunity to demonstrate knowledge and skills. Accommodations do not change the instructional level, content, or performance criteria for meeting the standards. Examples of accommodations include enlarging the print, providing Braille versions, testing orally, and using calculators.

A *modification* is a change in what a student is expected to learn and/or demonstrate. Although a student might be working on modified course content, the subject area remains the same as the rest of the class. If the decision is made to modify the curriculum, it is done in a variety of ways, for a variety of reasons, with a variety of outcomes. Again, modifications vary according to the situation. Four modification techniques are:

- *Same, Only Less:* The assignment remains the same, except the number of items are reduced. The items selected should be representative areas of the curriculum. For example, a social studies test might consist of multiple-choice questions, each with five possible answers. This test could be modified so that the number of possible answers is reduced to two.
- *Streamline the Curriculum:* The assignment is reduced in size, breadth, or focus to emphasize the key points. For example, in a language arts class, students might create an author study on Patricia Polacco with a journal on themes and impressions of the books they read. A student with a disability might focus on identifying the themes of the books he or she reads, and then create a display that uses pictures to support his or her writing on those main ideas.
- *Same Activity with Infused Objective:* The assignment remains the same, but additional components (such as IEP objectives or skills) identified are incorporated. This is often done in conjunction with other accommodations and/or modifications to ensure that all IEP objectives are addressed. For example, if a student has an IEP objective to answer factual and inferential questions, the math teacher might need to remember to ask these types of questions so that the student can practice this skill in a natural setting.

- *Curriculum Overlapping:* The assignment in one area may be completed during another time. Some students work slowly and need more time to complete assignments while others need to explore the connections between various content areas. For example, if a student participated in a poster project in his or her cooperative learning group during math centers, the product could also be used during language arts.

Deciding which technique to use depends on the type of assignment and the specific student. One assignment might only need to be reduced in size in order for the student to be successful, but another assignment might incorporate infused objectives. Each technique, as well as appropriate personal supports, should be considered for each situation. Remember that curriculum does not always need to be modified—even when considering students with more significant disabilities. When general education teachers provide multilevel instruction, changes to a lesson might not be necessary. Differentiating instruction allows all students a variety of ways to demonstrate knowledge while continuing to meet the requirements of the class. At other times, the curriculum can be made more accessible through accommodations and modifications. Table 8.1 lists additional curriculum accommodations and modifications.

Table 8.1. Accommodations and Modification Ideas

Ideas for Use with Instructional Materials

- Provide a calculator
- Supply graph paper to assist in organizing and lining up math problems
- Audio or video tape lectures
- Allow film or video and supplements or in place of text
- Provide practices opportunities using games, computers, language master, oral drills, and board work
- Offer a personal dry erase board
- Create a larger work space
- Use larger tools such as paint brushes
- Allow student to record thoughts and write while listening to audiotape or watching a video of the lecture or class assignment
- Provide visual aids to stimulate ideas
- Use an overhead projector to enlarge text and/or directions
- Allow the use of computers for writing
- Provide student with ink stamps for numbers, letters, date, and signature
- Tape the assignment to the desk or provide a clipboard that can be clamped to the desk or wheelchair tray to secure papers
- Use print enlarger or light box to illuminate text
- Use tactile materials
- Find accompanying enrichment materials on the student's reading level
- Use adapted computer hardware or software

Table 8.1.   Accommodations and Modification Ideas (continued)

Ideas for Use with In-Class Activities

- Break down new skills into small steps
- Simplify instruction by demonstrating and guiding learning one step at a time
- Repeat instructions as needed
- Role play historical events
- Underline or highlight important words and phrases
- Group students into pairs, threes, fours, etc. for different assignments and activities
- Pair students with different and complementary skills
- Pick key words from book to read on each page
- Turn pages in book while others read
- Rewrite text or use easy to read versions
- Use tape recorders for journal entries
- Have student complete sentences supplied by the teacher orally or in writing
- Supply incomplete sentences for student to fill in appropriate words or phrases
- Engage student in read, write, pair, share activities
- Use movement, pantomime, and sound patterns to interpret poetry, historical events, etc.
- Use hands-on, whole body (TPR) activities
- Color code important words or phrases

Ideas for Use with Projects or Homework

- Assign smaller quantities of work
- Relate problems to real-life situations
- Highlight problems to be completed
- Read problems and equations aloud
- Allow more time for completion
- Provide study questions, song texts, scripts, etc. in advance of an assignment
- Encourage oral contributions
- Assign concept maps and character webs
- Provide sample sentences for student to use as a model while writing
- Dictate report to a partner who writes it out or types it on the computer
- Assign homework partners
- Assign group projects to illustrate or perform a story setting (collages and dioramas)
- Substitute projects for written assignments and reports
- Use complementary software or adapted computer hardware
- Organize pictures instead of words into categories

Ideas for Use with Assessments

- Underline or highlight test directions
- Read word problems aloud
- Re-write problems using simpler language
- Underline key words
- Space problems further apart on the page
- Reduce the number of questions by selecting representative items
- Permit oral responses
- Put choices for answers on index cards

- Use the sentence or paragraph as a unit of composition rather than an essay
- Allow oral responses to tests using a tape recorder
- Use photographs in oral presentations to the class
- Re-word test questions in easier terms
- Assign final group projects with each student responsible for specific roles
- Encourage the use of other media for final products (film, video, audio, photos, drawings, performances, etc.)

CONCLUSIONS

Many of the supports that diverse learners require can be provided as part of the instructional arrangements in the classroom. Several years of research suggests that these instructional strategies are beneficial for all students, not only those who are identified as gifted, English language learners, or those with disabilities. Taken together, curriculum and instruction supports address many of the support needs for diverse learners.

Questions for further discussion, study, and project development:

- Describe how you will ensure that all students in your class can participate in your integrated arts lessons.
- Select two instructional strategies identified in this chapter and describe how they will be used in the lessons you have created during your work in previous chapters of this book.
- Describe the differences between accommodations and modifications for students with disabilities. Identify some of the ideas you could implement with students in your class.

CHAPTER 9

How Can I Assess Student Learning within Integrated Arts Lessons?

Learning is movement from moment to moment.

—J. Krishnamurti

The preceding chapters of this book have: covered the role of integrated arts teaching and learning toward the development of arts-loving readers; described standards within the four arts disciplines; defined various forms of content area integration with and through the arts; and offered ideas within direct teaching models for integrated arts curriculum at the elementary and middle school levels. However, at the core of our professional existence is the pressing need to not only clearly articulate why, what, and how we will teach, but also how we will determine if the students have learned what we have taught them. Forms of valuable assessment within integrated arts teaching are not impossible; in fact, they can become a welcomed addition to our efforts in developing arts-loving readers.

This chapter begins with the types of assessment with focus on the learners and doers—our students. In their book, *Performance-Based Curriculum for Music and the Visual Arts: From Knowing to Showing,* authors Helen Burz and Kit Marshall (1999) center their discussion of authentic assessment in the arts by first calling attention to the actions of the learner within an arts activity or experience. Within this book's graphic figure, "Learning Actions Wheel," the student is placed at the center of the wheel and presented (by the teacher) with a:

stimulus for learning. That stimulus may be an issue, idea, or question that may have been suggested to the teacher by the content standards (arts and other subjects), or it may be something of particular interest to the learner. The learner is in the center because no matter how important

we think the content is, it is inert until we add action to it. Everything re-
volves around the developmental levels, the motivation, and the engagement of the learner in the learning actions. (p. 6)

In other words, students in our classes may be presented with a challenge, project, or an action to take concerning arts integration learning. For
instance, if the students have read a book about a particular artist, they can
then be shown a work of art and are asked questions about color, line,
form, and brush technique. We then might ask what they see or know about
the content or subject matter of that painting and its connection to a piece
of recorded music, book they read, or poetry about the same theme, etc.
What is important here is that students within these integrated teaching
contexts would know they were about to be invited to actually "do" something to further that learning through their direct participation in creative
action directly involving them as artists, musicians, dancers, or actors.

Those student learning actions can include direct engagement within
what Burz and Marshall classify as the "Five Major Learning Actions
of a Performance" (p. 7). It is important that although the aforemen-
tioned authors are primarily concerned with the content and assessment
of two arts—visual art and music—the same perimeters are easily
adaptable to include learning and assessment (including drama and
dance). Additionally, while we know most of our integrated arts teaching in the general classroom will not result in formalized arts performances and/or exhibitions, we would like to suggest that the act of participation and learning as a student artist naturally involves sharing the
processes and making of that art, as well as the art work, music, drama,
or dance project itself. These informal and formal opportunities to
"show" what the students have learned can take place in a variety of
ways, every day within our own classrooms.

Following the outline Burz and Marshall provide, those student
learning actions include:

ACCESSING

The arts task, project, or performance begins with an interesting prompt
or question from the teacher. For instance, students might be asked to
discuss the "movement" they hear or imagine in a haiku, or see in a
Japanese watercolor of a natural scene related to that haiku theme (see
chapter 4). The students could be prompted to experiment (within small
cooperative groups) with creative movements to various spoken haiku

text and charged with the task of developing a mini-performance of that poem within painted scenery and created natural settings. Students will need to carefully access what they need to know to create a performance.

In our haiku example, the students gather needed information in a variety of ways—from the teacher's direct model; from provided Japanese art and haiku poetry books; from their previous experiences with video, art works, and literature about the culture, people, and stories of Japan; from appropriate authentic recorded music and instruments provided, etc. The students will be engaged in actions of observation, discussion, investigation, and experimentation as they begin the arts task ahead.

INTERPRETING

During our example, students will also be actively involved in actions of analyzing, comparing, contrasting, and categorizing in order to problem-solve and make decisions about their performance project. As they do so, students will be engaged in actions where they must consider which information they use, ignore, change, or alter. When students are asked to make art or perform, they are being asked to "analyze, compare, contrast, and categorize—to somehow meaningfully organize the information to represent what we think it all means" (p. 7).

Within our haiku performance example, students are engaged in this interpreting learning action stage as they experiment and decide on the most effective and expressive ways to organize their mini-performance. This is an extremely active (and many times, nonverbal) stage of the young students' creative process where decisions are made in a rapid succession of experimental phases. Student artists are considering many different avenues of expression, as well as considering and rejecting the thoughts and ideas of others in their cooperative group (sometimes rather ungraciously!) Structure is needed in terms of clearly defined artistic tasks, time and space perimeters, and guidelines and checkpoints concerning group expectations, behavior, and personal accountability.

PRODUCING

At this point, the groups have actively experimented and considered many options toward their mini-performance. What emerges now is a production component or learning action phase where students translate what they have learned into a useful and purposeful representation of the larger learning at hand. In other words, our haiku groups are now representing what they know about the art of haiku through a purposeful design to their performance, a construction that draws upon the students' composite learning. The learners are actually asking themselves and other group members several questions that are often unspoken and processed quickly. These include tacit questions about the best ways to show what the group knows and what the impact of those decisions could be on their audience. The group has much to consider.

DISSEMINATING

The fourth stage of learning action includes the actual performance, display, or sharing of the project or task. In our haiku example, students are excited to finally perform, as well as view others' creative work. At this point, learners are asked to share and communicate what they have learned and/or made with one or more others. In these authentic contexts (in which performance art involves an interested audience), learners become highly motivated to show and demonstrate what they have actively learned and created within particular performance settings.

The nature of performance motivation should not be underestimated as a powerful learning tool within integrated arts curriculum in the general classroom. Opportunities for performance sharing have been frequently and consistently cited throughout many of the previous chapters of this book and include some of the following: in-class performances in music, dance, and drama; cross-grade performance sharing of literature-based, themed integrated arts projects; displays of student artwork and journal writing/poetry; creative movement and drama presentations, performances of poetry with movement and drama, school-wide festivals and theme celebrations; student projects based on famous works of art, music, drama, and dance; and community service projects and outreach based on students' integrated arts projects.

EVALUATING

This important stage of active learning could occur throughout the other stages, but is typically an indication of the end of a performance cycle, or the beginning of yet another cycle of learning. The learners are asked to consider how things went, develop judgment and valuing of their own and others' efforts, and formulate plans to improve in the next effort. Important here is the choice of criteria (used in different ways throughout all the learning stages) that will be used to guide students' evaluations of their own and others' efforts. The overall goal here is for the teacher to design ways for the learners to engage in continuous self and group evaluation on a day-by-day basis so that evaluation of arts learning becomes as natural an activity as the creative processes of making that art. Thus, evaluation and assessment (the word *assessment* originally meant to sit beside, as in acts of reflection and dialogue with others) is a natural and cyclical activity designed to improve instruction, learning, and a student's sense of self-efficacy through continuous reflection, discussion, judgement, reevaluation, and experimentation with new learning. The role of the teacher is to ask important questions, encourage student's self-assessment through reflection activity and informed judgement, and provide feedback to the learner (and among learners) toward the improvement and encouragement of their creative and artistic efforts.

The following list describes several ideas and suggestions for assessment and evaluation activities of integrated arts learning based on criteria embedded within arts standards and standards within multiple subjects.

EXAMPLES OF ASSESSMENT MATERIALS AND PROCEDURES FOR INTEGRATED ARTS

The purpose of this section is to add to the discussion of possibilities for valid and accurate assessments of active integrated arts learning within our general classrooms. Although we know educators already know how to create effective quizzes and essays for content-area assessments, creative tools for active, purposeful authentic assessment of learning with and through the arts can include more than traditional quizzes, tests, and other written measurements. The following are several examples of assessment tools linked to the arts standards that are appropriate for use within integrated arts learning activity.

Speaking Checklist

As noted, literacy involves viewing, reading, writing, listening, and speaking. However, public speaking is often forgotten or neglected—especially for students acquiring English as a second language. To focus more attention on the use of oral language skills in the classroom, we suggest that teachers use a speaking checklist similar to the one in table 9.1. Teachers use this in a variety of ways. In some classrooms, teachers require students to do presentations while being evaluated by their peers. These students have time during class to work on their presentations, receive feedback on the development of content and process from their teacher, and incorporate information into their sessions. Other teachers encourage their students to present information to younger grades. For example, a sixth grade teacher might arrange for her students to present to third and fourth graders. The speaking checklist, therefore, would be completed by the teacher of the younger students and provided to the presenter. In other classrooms, this assessment is much less formal and is conducted on an individual basis. Students may receive feedback on their speaking skills during small group lessons, class interactions, as well as

Table 9.1.   Speaking Checklist

Name: _____

When _____ speaks in a group, he/she:

	Sept.	Dec.	Mar.	June
sticks to the topic.				
builds support for the subject.				
speaks clearly.				
takes turns and waits to talk.				
talks so that others in the group can hear.				
speaks smoothly.				
uses courteous language.				
presents in an organized and interesting way.				
supports the topical thesis.				
answers questions effectively.				
is comfortable speaking publicly.				
maintains listeners' interest.				
volunteers to answer in class.				

A = always, S = sometimes, N = never

interactions on the playground or in various other communicative settings. When using the speaking checklist, teachers and students should add the additional behaviors that they wish to observe and expand.

A focus on the development of students' oral language skills (exercised during student speeches and oral reports) can be easily adapted to student learning and speaking within integrated arts contexts. For instance, if a teacher wishes to use speaking checklist assessment during classroom activities where students present individual or group oral reports about favorite paintings or other works of art, the checklist might be customized to include some of the following categories:

- Shows or points out components of the painting discussed
- Adds to the class knowledge base about the painter and painting by using new vocabulary
- Uses teminology about art learned in class: line, form, shape, texture, etc.
- Compares and contrasts the work of art to another work by this or another artist

Drama and music offer important ways for students to use language in highly expressive and meaningful contexts. What is important is that the arts offer multiple, direct avenues of opportunities toward the development of students' skills in speaking, which are vitally linked to their development as readers and writers.

Knowledge Charts

Inherent in building upon any content area knowledge base is the learners' need to find a voice to express what they already know, what they would like to know, and how they might learn more. Active learning with and through the arts includes important episodes where students are asked to discuss, actively list, or check off vocabulary, elements, and concepts about the art or arts they are studying. Toward purposes outlined in previous chapters, this development of artistic perception must include the ability to actively use and apply elements and vocabulary descriptive of the art in which the students are engaged with links to their reading and language development.

Simply put, our students need to be able to communicate about their arts experiences by using concepts and words that are unique to the arts. These elements might first manifest themselves within the student's awareness of sensory information—how a piece of music sounds, what a dance communication evokes, the characteristics of the media used in a work of visual art, or understanding the dramatic context of a play— which then find a voice through students' attempts to use the descriptive terminology embedded in each of the arts.

In an integrated arts unit about string instruments, musicians, and music (see chapter 6), the students were asked to fill in a vocabulary chart about what they already knew about each musical term, what they then found out, and where they learned that new information (see table 9.2). This chart was used by students throughout their book-club activity and video viewing about strings and string musicians. As the students worked in small cooperative groups, they kept their individual knowledge charts

Table 9.2.   Let's Find Out About Strings (Vocabulary Chart)

Word	What I Think It Means	What It Really Means	Where I Found Out
strings			
bow			
tuning			
pegs			
fingerboard			
bridge			
sound hole			
plucked			
string family			
violin			
viola			
cello			
double bass			
fiddle			
string section			
orchestra			
rehearsal			
performance			

nearby. Some groups decided to submit their chart as a group effort; other groups decided to keep this assessment activity as an individual effort.

What is important here is that the students were actively engaged in a written assignment that structured and motivated their curiosity and vocabulary development about the learning at hand. They were challenged to learn more and write what they were learning on their chart. Because the students knew this assignment would become one of the formal assessments of their learning within the string unit, this assessment activity became vitally woven into the fabric of the arts instruction.

In a middle elementary grade arts activity, students were asked to compare one dance activity (square dance) to another (their creative, improvised movement to twentieth-century recorded music). To do so, the teacher realized that the students needed to revisit each dance context, giving the students time to discuss, reflect, and write about elements of each. After the students performed the first dance, the teacher gave each student labeled colored cards on which to write their own descriptive words about the use of energy and force, direction, shape, form, style, and music used in each dance. Students were asked to discuss their cards with one other student, then two others. Each group of four was then asked to create a large paper chart with each of the card categories listed. They were to agree on the best way to describe each category of the dance, and sign their chart (for final assessment and grading purposes).

After this phase of small group work, the teacher then had the entire class perform the same dance again, meet in their small cooperative groups again, and finally present their descriptive charts to the whole class. The same procedure was followed for the twentieth-century dance piece. After both sets of charts were made, the teacher led a lively discussion about similarities and differences in each dance. Vocabulary about dance was developed by students applying appropriate language to the direct actions of making art within an active assessment activity.

In an upper elementary and middle school unit pairing children's literature with listening to authentic recorded samples of jazz (McDonald, Fisher, and Helzer, in press), students were introduced to poetry, stories, and vocabulary about jazz and jazz musicians through directed musical listening. After learning about the sound characteristics of each of the categories within their "Listening to Jazz Checklist" (see table 9.3), students were asked to first make decisions about a sample of recorded music together, as a whole group. The students first listened to the recorded sample and checked off their own opinions and judgments about that sample.

Table 9.3. Listening to Jazz Checklist

Instruments	Rhythm Section	Style	Tempo	Dynamics	Improv	Artist Name
• Piano	• Walking bass line	• Pre-jazz (West African, work songs, spirituals, New Orleans, ragtime)	• Fast	❑ Loud	❑ Solo	❑
• Bass	• Pattern on high hat	• Early blues	• Medium	❑ Medium	❑ Solo within the group	❑
• Drums	• Chatter on snare	• Blues (country blues, delta blues guitar, others)	• Slow	❑ Soft	❑ Solo with rhythm section	❑
• Assorted percussion	• Others:	• Chicago stride	• Fast to slow	❑ Changing (how?)	❑ Playing in the moment (all improvised)	
• Sax		• Swing (vocal/instrumental)	• Slow to fast			
• Clarinet		• Scat	• Changes (how?)			
• Other winds		• Bebop				
• Guitar		• Fusion				
• Electronic or computerized		• Funk				
• Others:		• Latin jazz				
		• Others:				

The sample was played again and the checklist was used as an overhead projection activity in which the teacher or a student checked off the class decisions (based on lively large-group discussion and repeated playings of the recording) within each descriptive category. After multiple applications of this checklist to class jazz-listening activities (to many recorded samples of jazz and other music), the teacher was then able to naturally, easily, and effectively use this familiar assessment tool for individual and small-group formal written assessments. The teacher thereby structured the students' ability to focus on what they were hearing in their musical listening.

PERFORMING ARTS OR VISUAL ART FEEDBACK ASSESSMENT

One of the joys of choosing to incorporate the arts as an active way of teaching and learning within multiple contexts is to involve our students as educated audiences and viewers of the arts. Although we firmly believe that art should be performed and viewed, enjoyed, valued, and esteemed for its own intrinsic experiential worth, the realities and challenges of student focus and behavior shape our need to structure the young audience experience into meaningful and educational contexts. One way to structure a meaningful assessment activity stemming from art-performance experiences is to create a class rubric or writing prompt to guide how students will view and value that art experience.

After viewing a traveling high school play and meeting several student performers, young students were asked to use the following writing prompts and rubric to rate their overall experience in viewing the play.

Here are examples of discussion and writing prompts used to illicit student reactions and responses.

- Describe the plot or storyline of the play. What was the play about? What happened?
- Describe your favorite character. What did he/she do? How did he/she change during the play? What situations did he/she experience? Why did you like this character?
- Describe one favorite scene in the play. Name the characters involved, what happened, and how you felt about this action.
- Draw one of the play's scenery backdrops. Describe its importance to the play.
- Describe one of the following: favorite costumes, lighting effects, sound effects, surprise event, movement, or props. How did this add to the play?

- On a scale of 1 to 5 (5 being best), rate the following:
  Script and story line: _____
  Actors: _____
  Action: _____
  Scenery: _____
  Lighting: _____
  Costumes: _____
  Props: _____
  Overall, I would rate this audience experience as a _____
  because _____.

What is important here is that these assessments were created by young students through direct input in class discussions; therefore, their terminology reflects their current class level of vocabulary about the elements of drama. Because the students were invested in the creation of the actual assessment tool, they were more than willing to carry a pencil and fill in information about their experiences.

The students were provided with opportunities to interview individual actors and the director of the high school play. They also knew their descriptive writing would be displayed on a class bulletin board alongside their own photos of the play and the young actors. Interestingly, many young students chose to be photographed next to their favorite high school actors. Additionally, the high school performers were structured and more focused in their responses to the students' questions about their play because of the younger students' use of these assessment tools.

INTEGRATED ARTS GROUPWORK:
GROUP PROGRESS CHECKS

Although we know that cooperative group work can serve as an active catalyst to heighten student interest and creativity involving learning with and through the arts, we have all also experienced the negative side of student small group experiences. Our young students can suffer the consequences of our unclear expectations, lack of or disorganization of time and space structures, as well as frequent off-task behavior of one or more group members. Severe examples of group work gone awry can include students who become angry, disengaged, and resentful of others, as well as students who dominate or control group decisions against the will of the majority. Because instructional goals of group work include the development of our students' social skills, abilities to debate and discuss, cooperate, make decisions, and choose right actions with others (citizenship), it is the teacher's responsibility to structure the experience for the students' benefit.

One way to structure group experiences and at the same time create a natural assessment tool is to initiate simple written group-progress checks where each member of the group receives the same grade as others in the group on each of their group progress reports or checks. During the time of class sessions devoted to small-group work, start the class by giving each group a printed progress check form to fill out and turn in within a specified time. Be sure the students know that these progress checks will be graded and will be part of their overall project or performance grade. The first progress check should be less specific than those that follow; each progress check should build upon the next toward the goals of the group project.

In a middle school social studies class, students were introduced to several cultures through the music, instruments, songs and dances, stories and legends, and examples of food from those selected world cultures. As an outgrowth of this learning, the teacher then assigned small groups of four to seven students a specific culture to research, create, and perform a multicultural music report. Resources such as maps, social studies texts, multicultural music recordings, simple world recipe books, visuals of instruments of many cultures, etc., were provided for the students to use.

Toward the creation and "performance" of this report, the students knew that two progress report checks would be due at specific times during their class-time research. The outline for the content of the first progress report appears in table 9.4.

The next progress report asked students to specify details of what would be performed or reported in each area and how. They were also asked to practice and time their report and record the results. It is important that once this teacher began the use of progress checks and the structure they helped provide, the level of student preparation and poise during the projects was greatly increased. In their self-assessments of this project, students repeatedly cited the progress check as the "thing that caused us to get going and stop wasting time." Thus, progress checks are teacher-created assessment tools that help focus, redefine, motivate, and structure group experiences to the benefit of each student.

STUDENT SELF-ASSESSMENT OF INTEGRATED ARTS ACTIVITY

Another way to collect information about students involves students' reflecting on their own habits. This assessment is useful in determining

Table 9.4.   Multicultural Music Project: Progress Check #1

Members of our group: _____, _____, _____,
_____, _____, _____, _____.

Culture: _____

Continent: _____

Hemisphere: _____

Language(s) Spoken: _____

Religion(s): _____

Approximate distance in miles from our city: _____

Please list who will be researching each area and the actual name of one book,
    Web site, CD, or other resource that the person intends to use:
Role of music in this culture:

Names of native instruments (two to three instruments):

Name of song or dance you will perform:

Name of story or legend you will read aloud or dramatize:

Name of food from this culture you will prepare and serve:

On the back of this page, create a paragraph that describes your report:

instructional priorities and in providing the student the opportunity to develop self-monitoring skills. A form similar to the one shown in table 9.5 could be completed by each child three or four times throughout the school year. In doing so, students could be encouraged to respond to more-specific questions and to analyze their interest and involvement in integrated arts. They might like to complete this alone or with a parent or teacher.

One example of the use of a self-assessment inventory within an integrated arts context included class learning activities where students had studied the work of Seurat (a French painter), created their own art representative of his style, and then viewed and discussed a video of a Broadway musical theatre performance of "Sunday in the Park with George" by Steven Sondheim (starring Bernadette Peters and Mandy Pantankin). The students had learned about Seurat's use of pointillism, an impressionistic technique of painting with dots of color. After the students viewed the video of the musical (which includes scenes of Seurat at work and a human tableau of his famous painting, "Sunday in the Park"), they discussed the use of drama, dance, and music to portray the work of the artist, and developed the characters important to

Table 9.5. Self-Assessment Inventory

Name: _____ Date: _____ Grade: _____

Color the one most like you.

How am I doing at:

	Super	Just OK	Needing practice
looking up and using terms and concepts in art, music, drama, and dance? I am	☺	☺	☹
using vocabulary about the arts as I speak, write, and read? I am	☺	☺	☹
writing a summary of a video or live performance of art? I am	☺	☺	☹
taking notes while viewing performances of art? I am	☺	☺	☹
asking questions of teachers or friends to improve my comprehension? I am	☺	☺	☹
comparing and contrasting works of art? I am	☺	☺	☹
underlining new words as I read for recall? I am	☺	☺	☹
gaining comfort speaking, writing, and reading about the arts? I am	☺	☺	☹

What type of help do I think I need?

Suerat's life and works. The students then completed a customized self-assessment inventory list that included the following arts-related categories (see table 9.5):

Students will enjoy responding to these questions, which also focus student attention and learning before, during, and after a performance or exhibition viewing of arts.

CONCLUSION

There are multiple opportunities for meaningful assessment within classroom integrated arts experiences. This chapter has provided many examples designed to assess student learning within arts and other content-area standards. We have also provided ideas for students to discuss, read, write about, and self-assess during active arts experiences. It is important here that arts assessments activities can be woven into students' direct engagement in making or producing art (authentic assessment). Arts assessment can also be designed to be a natural outgrowth of the students' listening and appreciation, audience participation, and viewing and evaluating works of art. In these ways, creative and purposeful integrated arts assessment can enhance the child's developing literacy skills as it creates more natural links to the current learning.

Questions for further discussion, study, and project development:

- Why should students be assessed?
- What types of assessment can be used during integrated arts activities?
- What kinds of assessment can be used after integrated arts activities?
- What types of assessment will you implement for the lesson you created earlier in this book?

CHAPTER 10

What Happens When They Go Home?

Living is a form of not being sure, not knowing what is next or how. The moment you know how, you begin to die a little. The artist never entirely knows. We guess. We may be wrong, but we take leap after leap in the dark.

—Agnes de Mille

HOW CAN I HELP FAMILIES NURTURE MY STUDENTS' INTEREST IN THE ARTS AND READING?

When students leave our classrooms at the end of the day, they aren't finished learning. We might not be directly responsible for their time, but we can influence and support their after-school activities. By partnering with families, we can ensure that all students are provided with opportunities to continue their learning into the community. This chapter provides teachers with several ideas that they can share with family members to ensure that students continue learning to read and to appreciate the arts beyond the traditional school day. The end of the chapter covers a specific resource that teachers and families can access.

READ-ALOUDS

Current research supports what parents have always known: reading aloud to children benefits their language development, acquisition of skills, social skills, and strengthens the parent–child bond. Even infants who are not yet able to process the content of what is being read and sung to them thrive on the physical contact and richness of language that comes with a read-aloud. We suggest that twenty minutes a day of "lap time" be set aside for a read-aloud at home by an adult caregiver or older sibling. It is important that children who have difficulty with maintaining attention for long periods of time can enjoy read-alouds that are broken into smaller segments. Chapter books are entertaining read-alouds for older children—even for those who are reading independently. Sharing one chapter per night before bedtime can serve as a quiet transition while creating quality time in busy schedules.

VISITS TO THE LIBRARY

Regular visits to the local public library provide children and their parents with access to a wide variety of books, videos, music, and audiotapes. We believe that every student should own and use a public library card. Family trips to the library convey the important message that reading is a valued activity in the family; it is an inexpensive outing for all members of the family to share and enjoy.

In addition to the time that children spend in the public library with their family, students should visit the school library to check out books at least once each week. They should also have access to a number of books in their classroom library that they can check out and take home. Books should be everywhere and students should have multiple opportunities to borrow these books and read them at home with their families.

SELECTING APPROPRIATE BOOKS

Readers love stories that contain characters which resemble themselves. Along with classics and other favorites, we recommend the use of stories that focus on issues of diversity, as well as differences in communication styles and abilities. These types of books give voice to all children. We believe that teachers should warn parents to be critical consumers of the books they select—literature should meet the criteria set for all books: well-written, fully developed characters involved in an engaging and entertaining story line. We hope that teachers will suggest the books on the arts and artists that were provided in chapter 6. These books provide children with glimpses into the lives of artists and allow them to see that their families value the arts as well.

As noted, we believe that there are several criteria for selecting books. First, books should be challenging, but not frustrating for students. Therefore, classroom and home libraries should contain books with a wide range of difficulty levels. This is especially helpful for students with disabilities and those less fluent in English. Second, we believe that classroom and home libraries should be filled with books that have received national awards, including the Caldecott and Newbery Awards (local bookstores have lists of these books). Third, we believe that the book collection must be multicultural. The best classroom and home libraries are filled with books about people from all walks of life.

DEDICATED READING TIME

Dedicated time for reading sets a positive example for children on the importance and value that the adults in their lives place on literacy. We recommend that each family member select his or her own materials to be read during this designated time. Many families read at their home on a regular basis. Some families choose other relaxing settings for this enjoyable activity, such as weekend visits to a local coffeehouse, a shady park, or the backyard patio. One family we know reads in the backyard several times a week and at the park every weekend.

ALTERNATE TEXT FORMATS

We suggest that teachers remind parents that less-fluent readers and students who are auditory learners can enjoy books on tape, picture books, or the comics section from the Sunday newspaper. The growing popularity of listening to audio recordings of books has led to a boom in the availability of a wide variety of bestsellers and classics. As well as an effective strategy for older students to complete literature course readings, it is also an enjoyable way to "read" books that a child might not currently have the skills to read independently. We also recommend that families who spend time in the car should choose a book for active listening or songs that allow for conversations afterward. Further, we encourage teachers to provide parents with questions about books and songs so that they can assist children in the comprehension of the story and its characters. Picture books and picture books with accompanying audiotapes, for younger readers, are becoming increasingly available. Children can listen repeatedly to old favorites while they follow along in the text.

Videotapes of books and stories are often overlooked as a tool for reading. As many teachers note, visual literacy is increasingly recognized as an important skill in today's multimedia society. Techniques for increasing visual literacy skills include reading a book first, then viewing the video version of the same book. After viewing the video, a discussion about the similarities and differences between the two is an especially helpful comprehension aid for many students. We suggest that teachers always inform parents of the books that their class is reading, the movies they see, and the performances they attend. When a video is available, we encourage teachers to allow parents to borrow it from the classroom library. Although it is often difficult, we suggest that teachers and parents stop the videotape from time to time and ask questions concerning comprehension (What just happened? Why did the boy do that?) and prediction (What do you think will happen next?). A child's familiarity with these questions will serve them well in their literacy acquisition.

PERFORMING AS A WAY TO LEARN

We know that students love to perform the stories that they are reading. We also know that comprehension for all students is enhanced when drama, music, and movement are used. Children who struggle with concepts of character development, sequence, and motivation can experience stories in other ways when performance techniques are used. For example, one teacher we know often uses a Reader's Theatre strategy in which students assume the roles of characters and recreate the dialogue from the text. Viewers follow along in the text to reinforce their own skills.

In addition to the time that students perform at school, we suggest that teachers inform parents of the community theatre and after-school program opportunities. These additional opportunities are selected by families for their reinforcement of the things students learn at school.

VISITS TO MUSEUMS

Many times parents do not have current information on museum collections or information about the use of these collections to supplement classroom instruction. This is especially the case if museums have "free–days," when community members can enter for free. A class newsletter could contain information about local museums and their permanent and traveling exhibits. Parents will especially appreciate tips on what to look for on museum visits. In fact, many teachers create short writing prompts and "museum viewing checklists" to share with parents—this often makes the trip to the museum more "educational" and might count as a homework make-up assignment.

For example, a fourth grade class was studying transportation. The teacher in this class included information about the free day at the local automobile museum in her regular parent newsletter. She suggested that parents show their children the different cars and then ask them to answer some specific questions about cars, such as "when was the Model T developed?" and "which was the oldest car you found in the museum?" The form then suggested that the student select two cars to write a compare/contrast paper about.

ATTENDING COMMUNITY ART EVENTS

Most communities provide its citizens with a wealth of cultural events; many parents understand the importance of these events to their children's development. However, some parents cannot easily access the wide range of plays, dance performances, film festivals, concerts, and puppet shows available. Thankfully, most community newspapers and arts councils produce a monthly or quarterly listing of events. Teachers can share this list with families and help them select appropriate events based on the students' age, the topics under study at school, and the resources available.

Again, teachers can ensure that these experiences connect with authentic learning by providing families with background information to discuss on the way to the event, questions to ask during intermissions, as well as prompts and activities to complete after the event. Although we do not believe that every cultural arts event must involve school work, we have learned from many families that conversation starters and prompts are helpful.

AT-HOME ART CENTER

One of the most interesting things that students tell us about making art is that they get in trouble from their parents when they do art at home. As teachers, you might want to suggest that families create a safe place for art making in their home, backyard, or garage. This area should contain all the supplies necessary for art making with space for working. We encourage families to allow their children to keep this area a bit messy—and not have strict rules about cleaning up before dinner, etc. This area could resemble an artist's workshop—it is neat when company visits, but most times it resembles organized chaos.

The supplies that children will need for their art making vary on the child's interests and needs. Most children will want traditional art supplies (such as paints, pastels, markers, paper, scissors, etc.). Some will want unique items (such as buttons, felt, pipe cleaners, etc.) for their creations. Still others will begin collecting "found items" that they can incorporate into their work. Given this complexity, parents might be encouraged to make or buy storage items so that some of the materials can be put away when they are not in use.

ART FOR GIFTS

One of the unique ways to encourage students to create art with their families is to encourage the giving of "homemade" gifts, rather than store-bought gifts. Children can be encouraged to make the presents that they give for holidays, birthdays, and other celebrations. Although many parents have never considered this, children naturally want to make things to give to adults. A simple conversation with families about the importance of art making and the positive reactions that children expect from adults will likely result in many families adopting this practice.

FURTHER RESOURCES FOR EDUCATION IN THE ARTS

The most comprehensive listing of information for advocacy and implementation of education in the arts at your school and community can be found within the umbrella Web site: www.aep-art.org. This is your best source of information. Within this site, educators and parents will find hundreds of items, including teaching resources, funding information, and materials to promote the important role of arts within education. Also included is valuable information on public awareness campaigns supporting arts education, list serves and discussion groups, and an expansive state and national arts agency directory. Simply put, you will find everything you need at this site.

According to the information found within that site:

> The **Arts Education Partnership** (formerly the *Goals 2000 Arts Education Partnership*) is a national coalition of arts, education, business, philanthropic and government organizations that demonstrates and promotes the essential role of the arts in the learning and development of every child and in the improvement of America's schools. The Partnership includes over 140 organizations that are national in scope and impact. It also includes state and local partnerships focused on influencing education policies and practices to promote quality arts education. Partnership organizations affirm the central role of imagination, creativity and the arts in culture and society; the power of the arts to enliven and transform education and schools; and collective action through partnerships as the means to place the arts at the center of learning.
>
> The Arts Education Partnership was formed in 1995 through a cooperative agreement among the National Endowment for the Arts (NEA), the United States Department of Education (USDE), the National Assembly of State Arts Agencies (NASAA), and the Council of Chief State School Officers (CCSSO).

Also available at this Web site are important publications that easily and effectively describe the role of arts in the curriculum and the effect of education in the arts on student learning and achievement. Among the most requested publications are: *Champions of Change: The Impact of the Arts on Learning, Gaining the Arts Advantage: Lessons from School Districts that Value Arts Education, Learning Partnerships: Improving Learning in Schools with Arts Partners in the Community* (an interactive Web site publication), *Young Children and the Arts: Making Creative Connections, Good Schools Require the Arts* (available in PDF format only). These and other publications are also available by writing, calling, or faxing the following organization:

Arts Education Partnership
One Massachusetts Ave., NW, Ste. 700
Washington, D.C. 20001-1431
Information line: (202) 326-8693
Fax number: (202) 408-8081

Within this Web site is, a twelve-minute video and advocacy kit described in the following way:

> **The Arts and Children: A Success Story** (1996) A 12-minute video featuring actress Meryl Streep that demonstrates the impact of quality arts education on student academic and personal achievement. Includes a kit with handouts summarizing current arts education research and national policies and legislation, the brochure Eloquent Evidence, tips on how to use the video in a public awareness campaign, and more. $19.95, price does not include shipping costs. Available from the National Assembly of State Arts Agencies, phone: (202) 347-6352, and Americans for the Arts, phone: (800) 321-4510 ext. 241.

CONCLUSION

A love of reading and the arts is first developed in the home, where parents play a powerful role teaching their children the importance of literacy, learning, and expression. It is never too early to begin reading and singing to babies, and the practice of reading aloud can extend beyond the time when a child can read independently. We know that strategies used at home support school instruction. We also know that families serve as a valuable and knowledgeable collaborator for teachers and we encourage teachers to tap into this most valuable resource.

Questions for further discussion, study, and project development:

- Why should families participate in community arts events with their children?

- What are some messages about the arts that you would like to send to families of the children in your class?
- Design a class newsletter that informs families about the integrated arts activities occurring in your classroom and school. Include information about community arts events that relate to these school-based activities.
- Identify three arts events occurring within your community over the next three months and describe why families should participate in these events. Create a simple discussion guide for students to use with their families. Also design several writing prompts for students and families to record their reflections and reactions to arts events.

Bibliography

Abouzeid, M. P., Invernizzi, M. A., Bear, D., and Ganske, K. (2000). "Word sort: Approaching phonics through spelling." *The California Reader*, 33(4), 21–28.

Adams, M. J. (1998). *Phonemic awareness in young children*. Baltimore: Paul H. Brookes.

Adams, P. (1999). *There was an old lady who swallowed a fly*. New York: Child's Play International.

Asher, J. J. (1996). *Learning another language through actions (Fifth Ed.)*. Los Gatos, Calif.: Sky Oaks Productions.

August, D., and Hakuta, K. (Eds.). (1998). "Educating language-minority children." Washington, D.C.: National Academy Press.

Barrett, J. (2001). "Interdisciplinary work and musical integrity." *Music Educators Journal*, 87(5), 27–31.

Barrett, J., McCoy, C., and Veblen, K. (1997). *Sound ways of knowing: Music in the interdisciplinary curriculum*. New York: Schirmer Books.

Barry, N. (1998). "Arts integration in the elementary classroom: Conference development and evaluation." *Update: Applications of Research in Music Education,* 17(1), 3–8.

Bauer, C. F., (Ed.) (1988). *Windy day: Stories and poems*. New York: Lippincott.

Baum, S. M., Olenchak, F. R., and Owen, S. V. (1998). "Gifted students with attention deficits: Fact and/or fiction? Or, can we see the forest for the trees?" *Gifted Child Quarterly*, 42(2), 96–104.

Berghoff, B. (2001). "Going beyond words." *Primary Voices K–6*, 9(4), 34–37.

Booth, D. (1985). "Imaginary gardens with real toads? Reading and drama in education." *Theory Into Practice*, 24, 193–198.

Booth, J. (1994). *Big bugs: Getting to know the little creatures up close*. San Diego: Harcourt Brace.

Broudy, H. (1984). *A rationale for the arts as general education*. Summer Institute for Educators, Music Center Education Division, Los Angeles.

Bulloch, I. (1994). *Patterns*. London: Thomson Learning.

Burns, M. (1995). *The greedy triangle*. New York: Scholastic.

Burz, H. L., and Marshall, K. (1999). *Performance-based curriculum for music and the visual arts: From knowing to showing*. Thousand Oaks, Calif.: Corwin Press.

Busching, B. A. (1981). "Readers theatre: An education for language and life." *Language Arts*, 58, 330–338.

Cairney, T. H. (1996). "Pathways to meaning making: Fostering intertextuality in the classroom." In L. B. Gambrell and J. F. Almasi (Eds.), *Lively discussions: Fostering engaged reading* (pp. 170–180). Newark, Del.: International Reading Association.

California Department of Education (1999). *Reading and Language Arts Framework for California Schools*. Sacramento: California Department of Education.

California Department of Education. (1996). *Visual and performing arts framework for California public schools: Kindergarten through grade twelve*. Sacramento: California Department of Education.

Campbell, P. S., and Scott-Kassner, C. S. (1995). *Music in childhood: From preschool through the elementary grades*. New York: Schirmer.

Carle, E. (1973). *I see a song*. New York: Scholastic.

Carpenter, M. C. (1998). *Halley came to Jackson*. New York: HarperCollins.

Clay, M. (1985). *The early detection of reading difficulties* (3rd ed.). Auckland, New Zealand: Heinemann.

Cohn, A. (1993*). From sea to shining sea: A treasury of American folklore and folk songs*. New York: Scholastic.

Colbert, J., and Harms, A., (Eds.) (1998). *Dear Dr. King: Letters from today's children to Dr. Martin Luther King, Jr.* New York: Hyperion.

Consortium of National Art Education Associations (American Alliance for Theatre and Education, Music Educators National conference, National Art Education Association, National Dance Association) (1994). *National standards for arts education: Dance, music, theatre, visual arts: What every young American should know and be able to do in the arts*. Reston, Va.: Music Educators National Conference.

Cooney, B. (1982). *Miss Rumphius*. New York: Viking Press.

Cox, C. (1998). *Children's stance towards literature: A longitudinal study, K–5*. Paper presented at the 1998 American Educational Research Association, San Diego.

Cox, C., and Many, J. E. (1992). "Stance toward a literary work: Applying the transactional theory to children's responses." *Reading Psychology*, 13, 37–72.

Dahl, K. L., and Farnan, N. (1998). *Children's writing: Perspectives from research*. Newark, Del.: International Reading Association.

De Angeli, M. (1989). *The door in the wall*. New York: Doubleday.

Dugan, S., and Desir, L. (1998). "Ethnography and 'Lucy': ESL students in the 'content' class." *Research and Teaching in Developmental Education*, 14(2), 51–57.

Egan, J., (Ed.) (1999). *Solar system*. New York: Golden Books Publishing.

Ehri, L. C., Nunes, S. R., Willows, D. M., Schuster, B. V., Yaghoub-Zadeh, Z., and Shanahan, T. (2001). "Phonemic awareness instruction helps children learn to read: Evidence from the National Reading Panel's meta-analysis." *Reading Research Quarterly*, 36, 250–283.

Eisner, E. (1980). "The arts as a way of knowing." *Principal*, 60(1), 11–14.

Eisner, E. (1983). "The invention of mind: Technology and the arts." *The Education Digest*, 49(1), 24–36.

Emberly, B. (1987). *Drummer hoff*. New York: Simon and Schuster.

Faltis, C. J., and Wolfe, P. M. (Eds.) (1998). *So much to say: Adolescents, bilingualism, and ELS in the secondary school*. New York: Teachers College.

Fearn, L., and Farnan, N. (1998). *Writing effectively: Helping children master the conventions of writing*. Boston: Allyn & Bacon.

Fisher, D., and Frey, N. (in press). *Responsive curriculum design in secondary schools: Meeting the diverse needs of students*. Lanham, Md.: Scarecrow Education.

Fisher, D., and McDonald, N. (2000). "With stars in their eyes: Deepening students' understanding of the bight sky." *Telling Stories: Theory, Practice, Interviews and Reviews The Journal of Teachers Encouraging a Love of Literature*, 4(2), 15–22.

Fisher, D., Flood, J., and Lapp, D. (1999). "Literature in the literacy process." In L. Gambrell, L. Morrow, S. Neuman, and M. Pressley (Eds.), *Best practices in literacy instruction* (pp. 119–135). New York: Guilford.

Fisher, D., Frey, N., and Sax, C. (1999). *Inclusive elementary schools: Recipes for success*. Colorado Springs, Colo.: PEAK Parent Center.

Fisher, D., Lapp, D., and Flood, J. (1999). "How is phonics really taught?" *The Yearbook of the National Reading Conference*, 48, 134–145.

Fisher, D., Pumpian, I., and Sax, C. (1998). "High school students' attitudes about and recommendations for their peers with significant disabilities." *Journal of the Association for Persons with Severe Handicaps*, 23, 272–282.

Fiske, E. (Ed.) (1999). *Champions of change; The impact of the arts on learning*. Washington, D.C.: The Arts Education Partnership and the President's Committee on the Arts and the Humanities. http://www.artsedge.kennedy-center.org/champions/

Fleischman, P. (1988). *Joyful noise: Poems for two voices*. New York: HarperTrophy.

Flood, J., Lapp, D., and Fisher, D. (in press). "Reading comprehension instruction." In J. Flood, J. M. Jensen, D. Lapp, and J. R. Squire (Eds.), *Handbook on research on teaching the English language arts*. Mahwah, N.J.: Earlbaum.

Ford, D. Y. (1998). "The underrepresentation of minority students in gifted education: Problems and promises in recruitment and retention." *Journal of Special Education*, 32, 4–14.

Ford, H. (1998). *The young astronomer*. New York: DK Publishing.

Fountas, I. C., and Pinnell, G. S. (1996). *Guided reading: Good first teaching for all children*. Portsmouth, N.H.: Heinemann.

Frey, N. (in press). "Standards-based lesson planning: Differentiating instruction for all learners." *TASH Yearbook*.

Frey, N., Fisher, D., Lapp, D., and Flood, J. (1999). "Literacy: Opening books for learning." In B. E. Buswell, C. B. Schaffner, and A. B. Seyler (Eds.), *Opening doors: Connecting students to curriculum, classmates, and learning*. (2nd ed., pp 20–23) Colorado Springs, Colo.: PEAK Parent Center.

Friedersdorf, M. (1997). *Where do falling stars go?* Orlando, Fla.: Peaceful Village Publishing.

Gardner, H. (1984). *Art, mind and brain: A cognitive approach to creativity*. New York: Basic Books.

Gardner, H. (1993a). *Frames of mind: The theory of multiple intelligences* (Tenth Anniversary Edition). New York: Basic Books.

Gardner, H. (1993b). *Multiple intelligences: The theory in practice*. New York: Basic Books.

Gilles, C., Andre, M., Dye, C., and Pfannenstiel, V. (1998). "Constant connections through literature: Using art, music, and drama." *Language Arts*, 76, 67–75.

Grout, D. (1973). *A history of music*. New York: W.W. Morton.

Hancock, M. (2000). *A celebration of literature and response: Children, books, and teachers in K–8 classrooms*. Upper Saddle River, N.J.: Prentice Hall.

Harris, J. J., III., and Ford, D. Y. (1999). "Hope deferred again: Minority students underrepresented in gifted programs." *Education and Urban Society*, 31, 225–237.

Hiatt, E. L., and Covington, J. (1991). "Identifying and serving diverse populations." *Update on Gifted Education*, 1(3), 1–37.

Hoban, T. (1986). *Shapes, shapes, shapes*. New York: Morrow.

Hort, L. (1991). *How many stars in the sky?* Tambourine.

Hughes, L. (1994). *The dream keeper and other poems*. New York: Knopf.

Indie, S. (1998). *Auntie*. Aiea, Hawaii: Island Heritage Publishers.

Jacobs, H. H. (1989). *Interdisciplinary curriculum: Design and implementation*. Alexandria, Va.: Association for Supervision and Curriculum Development.

Jacobs, H. H. (1997). *Mapping the big picture: Integrating curriculum and assessment K–12*. Alexandria, Va.: Association for Supervision and Curriculum Development.

Jensen, E. (2001). *Arts with the brain in mind*. Alexandria, Va.: Association for Supervision and Curriculum Development.

Jonas, A. (1987). *Reflections*. New York: Morrow.

Kennedy, C. H., and Fisher, D. (2001). *Inclusive middle schools*. Baltimore: Paul H. Brookes.

Koch, K., and Farrell, K. (1985). *Talking to the sun: An illustrated anthology of poems for young people*. New York: The Metropolitan Museum of Art.

Kusugak, M. A. (1993). *Northern lights: The soccer trails*. Toronto: Annick Press.

Lamme, L. (1990). "Exploring the world of music through picture books." *The Reading Teacher*, 44, 294–300.

Landis, B., and Carder, P. (1972). *The eclectic curriculum in American music education: Contributions of Dalcroze, Kodaly, and Orff*. Washington, D.C.: Music Education National Conference.

Lapp, D., and Flood, J. (1992). *Teaching reading to every child (Third Ed.)*. New York: Macmillan/McGraw-Hill.

Lapp, D., and Flood, J. (1997). "Where's the phonics? Making a case (again) for integrated code instruction." *The Reading Teacher*, 50, 696–700.

Lapp, D., Fisher, D., and Flood, J. (1999). "Integrating the language arts and content areas: Effective research-based strategies." *The California Reader*, 32(4), 35–38.

Lapp, D., Flood, J., and Fisher, D. (1999). "Intermediality: How the use of multiple media enhances learning." *The Reading Teacher*, 52, 776–780.

Lapp, D., Flood, J., and Goss, K. (2000). "Desks don't move—students do: In effective classroom environments." *Reading Teacher*, 54, 31–36.

Levene, D. (1993). *Music through children's literature: Theme and variations*. Englewood, Colo.: Teacher Ideas Press.

MacLachlan, P. (1985). *Sarah, plain and tall*. New York: Harper & Row.

Marshall, J. (1986). *Wings: A tale of two chickens*. New York: Viking.

Martinez, M., and Teale, W. H. (1988). "Reading in a kindergarten classroom library." *The Reading Teacher*, 41, 568–573.

McCaslin, N. (1990). *Creative drama in the classroom*. New York: Longman.

McDonald, N. (1999, November). *Enhancing literacy through music and movement*. Paper presented at the California Reading Association Conference, Long Beach, Calif.

McDonald, N. (2000). "Constructivist listening: Real-life classroom management and discipline concerns." *General Music Today*, 13(2), 3–7.

McDonald, N., and Fisher, D. (1999a). "Bug suites: An uncommonly integrated performance unit for fourth through eighth graders." *Telling Stories: Theory, Practice, Interviews, and Reviews*, 3(2), 17–25.

McDonald, N., and Fisher, D. (1999b). "Living haiku: Scenes of sound in motion." In S. Totten, C. Johnson, L. R. Morrow, and T. Sills-Briegel (Eds.), *Practicing what we preach: Preparing middle level educator* (pp. 273–275). New York: Falmer.

McDonald, N., and Fisher, D. (2000). "Tell them I sing: A dialogue on integrating curricula." *General Music Today*, 14(1), 13–18.

McDonald, N., Fisher, D., and Helzer, R. (in press). "Stories of jazz: Introductory listening activities using children's literature and authentic music samples." *Music Educators Journal*.

Meier, D. (1996). "Supposing that . . ." *Phi Delta Kappan*, 78, 271–276.

Milord, S. (1996). *Tales of the shimmering sky: Ten global folktales with activities*. Charlotte, Vt.: Williamson Publishing.

Murray, J. (1983). "Art, creativity, and the quality of education." In F. B. Tuttle, Jr. (Ed.), *Fine arts in the curriculum* (pp. 23–30). Washington, D.C.: National Education Association.

Music Educators National Conference (1994a). *Dance, music, theatre, visual arts: What every young American should know and be able to do in the arts: National standards for arts education*. Reston, Va.: Music Educators National Conference.

Music Educators National Conference. (1994b). *The school music program: A new vision: The K–12 national standards, preK standards, and what they mean to music educators*. Reston, Va.: Music Educators National Conference.

National Association of State Boards of Education (NASBE). (1995). *Winning ways: Creating inclusive schools, classrooms, and communities*. Report of the NASBE study group on special education. Washington, D.C.: Author.

National Council for Teachers of Mathematics. (2000). *Principles and standards for school mathematics*. Reston, Va.: NCTM.

Navasky, B. (1993). *Festival in my heart: Poems by Japanese children.* New York: Harry N. Abrams.

O'Brien, P. (2000). *Steam, smoke, and steel: Back in time with trains.* Watertown, Mass.: Charlesbridge.

Ogle, D. (1986). "K-W-L: A teaching model that develops active reading of expository text." *The Reading Teacher,* 39, 564–570.

Oughton, J. (1992). *How the stars fell into the sky: A Navajo legend.* Boston: Houghton Mifflin.

Paul, A. W. (1996). *The seasons sewn: A year in patchwork.* San Diego: Browndeer Press.

Peck, I. (2000). *The life and words of Martin Luther King Jr.* New York: Scholastic.

Perez, M., and Rius, M. (1998). *Stars and galaxies: Looking beyond the solar system.* Hauppauge, New York: Barron's Educational Series.

Peterson, J S., and Margolin, L. (1997). "Naming gifted children: An example of unintended 'reproduction.'" *Journal for the Education of the Gifted,* 21(1), 82–101.

Polacco, P. (2000). *The butterfly.* New York: Philomel.

Polacco, P. (1998). *The keeping quilt.* New York: Simon and Schuster.

Rappaport, D. (2001). *Martin's big words.* New York: Hyperion.

Richardson, J. S. (2000). *Read it aloud! Using literature in the secondary content classroom.* Newark, Del.: International Reading Association.

Rielly, E. J. (1988). "Reading and writing haiku in the classroom." *Children's Literature Association Quarterly,* 13(3), 111–114.

Ringgold, F. (1998). *My dream of Martin Luther King.* New York: Dragonfly.

Rohmann, E. (1994). *Time flies.* New York: Dragonfly.

Romero, M. K. (1994). "Identifying giftedness among Keresan Pueblo Indians: The Keres study." *Journal of American Indian Education,* 34(1), 35–58.

Rosen, M. (1993). *Little rabbit foo, foo.* New York: Alladin.

Rosenblatt, L. (1978). *The reader, the text, the poem: The transactional theory of the literary work.* Carbondale, Ill.: Southern Illinois University Press.

Rosenblatt, L. M. (1995). *Literature as exploration.* New York: Modern Language Association.

Sadker, D. (1999). "Gender equity: Still knocking at the door." *Educational Leadership,* 56(7), 22–26.

Sapon-Shevin, M. (1994a). "Why gifted students belong in inclusive schools." *Educational Leadership,* 52(4), 64–68, 70.

Sapon-Shevin, M. (1994b). *Playing favorites: Gifted education and the disruption of community.* New York: State University of New York.

Schecter, D. (1997). *Science art: Projects and activities that teach science concepts and develop process skills.* New York: Scholastic.

Siebert, D. (1990). *Train song:* HarperCollins.

Silver, Burdett, & Ginn (1995). *The music connection.* Parsippany, N.J.: Silver, Burdett, & Ginn.

Simon, S. (Ed.) (1995). *Star walk.* New York: Morrow Junior Books.

Sisk, D. A. (1994). "Bridging the gap between minority disadvantaged high potential children and Anglo middle class gifted children." *Gifted Education International*, 10(1), 37–43.

Smith, J. (2000). "Singing and songwriting support early literacy instruction." *The Reading Teacher*, 53, 646–649.

Snyder, S. (2001). "Connection, correlation, and integration." *Music Educators Journal*, 87(5), 32–39.

Stephens, D. (1994). "Learning that art means." *Language Arts,* 71, 34–37.

Strom, R. (1990). "Talented children in minority families." *International Journal of Early Childhood*, 22(2), 39–48.

Taback. S. (1999). *Joseph had a little overcoat.* New York:Viking.

Taback, S. (1997). *There was an old lady who swallowed a fly.* New York: Viking.

Tarlow, E. (1998). *Teaching story elements with favorite books.* New York: Scholastic.

Templeton, S. (1995). *Children's literacy: Contexts for meaningful learning.* Boston: Houghton Mifflin.

The Metropolitan Museum of Art. (1985). *Talking to the sun: An illustrated anthology of poems for young people.* New York: Author.

Tomlinson, C. A. (1999). *The differentiated classroom: Responding to the needs of all learners.* Alexandria, Va.: Association for Supervision and Curriculum Development.

Tompert, A. (1997). *Grandfather Tang's story.* Montclair, N.J.: Dragonfly.

U.S. Department of Education. (1999). *To assure the free appropriate public education of all children with disabilities (IDEA, Section 618).* Twenty-first annual report to Congress on the implementation of the Individuals with Disabilities Education Act. Washington, D.C.: Author.

Van Laan, N. (1990). *Possum come a-knockin'.* New York: Knopf.

Vygotsky, L. S. (1962). *Thought and language.* (Eugenia Hanfmann and Gertrude Vakar, Ed. and trans.) Cambridge, Mass.: MIT.

Vygotsky, L. S. (1978). *Mind in society: The development of higher mental psychological processes.* Cambridge, Mass.: Harvard University Press.

Walter, A. (1959). "Carl Orff's music for children." *The Instrumentalist*, 27.

Watts-Taffe, S., and Truscott, D. M. (2000). "Using what we know about language and literacy development for ESL students in the mainstream classroom." *Language Arts*, 77, 258–265.

Weiss, G. D., and Thiele, B. (1995). *What a wonderful world.* New York: Atheneum Books for Young Readers.

Weitzman, J. P., and Glasser, R. P. (1998). *You can't take a balloon into the Metropolitan Museum.* New York: Dial Books for Young Readers.

Weitzman, J. P., and Glasser, R. P. (2000). *You can't take a balloon into the National Gallery.* New York: Dial Books for Young Readers.

Westcott, N. (1987). *Peanut butter and jelly.* New York: Dutton.

Wiggins, R. A. (2001). "Interdisciplinary curriculum: Music educator concerns." *Music Educators Journal*, 87(5), 40–44.

Wilkinson, L. C., and Silliman, E. R. (2000). "Classroom language and literacy learning." In M. L. Kamil, P. B. Mosenthal, P. D. Pearson, and R. Barr (Eds.) *Handbook of reading research: Volume III* (pp. 311–335). Mahwah, N.J.: Lawrence Erlbaum.

Wood, A. (1984). *The napping house*. New York: Harcourt Brace.

Yaden, D., Jr., Smolkin, L., and Conlon, A. (1989). "Preschoolers' questions about pictures, print convention, and story text during reading aloud at home." *Reading Research Quarterly*, 24, 188–214.

Yell, M. L., Rogers, D., Rogers, E. L. (1998). "The legal history of special education: What a long, strange trip it's been!" *Remedial and Special Education*, 19, 219–228.

Yopp, H. K., and Yopp, R. H. (1997). *Oopples and boo-noo-noos: Songs and activities for phonemic awareness*. New York: Harcourt Brace.

Zilinsky, P. (1990). *The wheels of the bus*. New York: Dutton.

Zolotow, C. (1992). *The seashore book*. New York: HarperCollins.

About the Authors

Nan McDonald, Ed.D, is an associate professor and coordinator of music education at San Diego State University's School of Music and Dance. With more than twenty-eight years of teaching experience in preschool through university-level music and integrated arts, she is actively involved in the education of future arts specialists and classroom teachers. She offers ongoing integrated arts professional growth (integrated arts in the curriculum and English language development) for practicing teachers with the urban City Heights/SDSU K–16 Educational Pilot where she is the K–12 Integrated Arts Curriculum Director.

McDonald is the author of numerous articles in national and international arts education publications. She is a program author for Scott Foresman/Silver Burdett Music *"Making Music"* 2002, a K–8 national text series in music. In addition to her teaching and writing, Nan coauthored and performed professionally in more than 300 performances of "Literature Alive," a music, dance, and drama performance series designed to promote reading in the elementary school. She has served as the executive state vice president of the California Music Educators Association and is a frequent presenter at local, state, and national conferences in music, reading, integrated arts, and classroom management and discipline.

Douglas Fisher, Ph.D., is an associate professor in the College of Education, Department of Teacher Education at San Diego State University, where he teaches classes in English language development and literacy. His background includes adolescent literacy and instructional strategies for diverse student needs. He often presents at local, state, and national conferences and has published a number of articles on reading/literacy, differentiated instruction, accommodations, and curriculum development. He is the coauthor (with Nancy Frey) of *Responsive Curriculum Design in Secondary Schools: Meeting the Diverse Needs of Students* (also published by Scarecrow Education). He currently serves as the director of professional development for the City Heights Educational Pilot.